ENTERPRISE

AGILE

Practical insight and methods
for successful IT delivery

First edition published in 2008 in Great Britain by

BJSS Limited
Coronet House
Queen Street
Leeds
LS1 2TW
United Kingdom

Fifth edition, November 2016

ISBN: 978-0-9565371-2-6

BJSS is an award-winning delivery-focused IT and business consultancy with clients in both the public and private sectors and experience across a wide range of industries.

With over 20 years IT delivery, service management and advisory experience we are renowned for technical excellence, cost-effective delivery and our proven BJSS Enterprise Agile approach.

From offices across the UK and USA we provide a range of services spanning the solution delivery and service management lifecycle.

Our experience of successful enterprise-level software delivery and support has been used to formalise our Enterprise Agile approach. Combining the best features of a number of methods with extensive practical experience, BJSS Enterprise Agile provides an appropriate, pragmatic and proven route to successful and repeatable change and service delivery.

When our company was founded in 1993, one of our core principles was a total focus on delivery. In our constant search to continue to deliver on that vision, we have dedicated a great deal of effort to discovering what works, and what doesn't, when delivering and maintaining enterprise scale systems.

This book represents a distillation of hundreds of work years of real-world experience of creating industrial strength software for clients in some of the most demanding public and private sector environments.

In this latest edition we've added more thoughts about Service agility, and our approach to delivering service for products in an Agile delivery pipeline.

I hope you find something of value here and that we have helped encourage you to put into practice some of the techniques we describe.

Glynn Robinson

Managing Director, BJSS

November 2016

Table of Contents

3   A Pattern for Delivering Value   31

4   The Optimal Team   49

5   Effective Leadership   69

8 Engineering Quality Outcomes — 121

9 Service Agility — 143

1

The Agility Challenge

Irrespective of the nature of your organisation, the chances are you are grappling with the same challenge - how to more rapidly and reliably adapt to the changing demands of clients, consumers or citizens.

While the drive to do things faster, cheaper and better is not new, the number of sectors being disrupted by innovative commercial models powered by digital technologies is unprecedented. These inventive new offerings further increase the expectations of customers, driving organisations to quickly adapt their services, or risk becoming irrelevant.

INTRODUCTION

In the first edition of BJSS Enterprise Agile, published in 2008, we focused on the use of Agile techniques to deliver software projects. Since then we have delivered many more projects using our Enterprise Agile method.

In the era of digital transformation, Agility is no longer the preserve of software development teams. It is increasingly important that the entire organisation functions in an Agile manner and is capable of rapid change.

The dynamic nature of global markets and recent technology innovations have prompted us to update our approach. In this revised edition we look not only at the software delivery lifecycle but also the wider subject of building and running technology-led products and services in an Agile organisation. This expanded scope includes areas such as integrating business change, service management, Cloud and software-defined infrastructure.

We have significantly expanded the scope of our method, but the underlying principles remain:

1. An absolute focus on high quality delivery.

2. A risk-first approach to prioritising delivery and change.

3. Strong architecture and engineering principles at the core.

4. Using only 'Necessary and sufficient' processes and artefacts.

5. Delivering change with a 'No surprises end-game'.

We explore current concepts, outline our views and experience and present our approach for successful delivery. Our aim is to help all organisations to address the Agility challenge with a focus on the delivery of high quality technology-led products and services.

CONCEPTS

DIGITAL TRANSFORMATION AS A DRIVER FOR AGILITY

The rise of digital technologies has been a key catalyst for increased Agility. Social media enables near instant feedback - making or breaking products and services overnight. Consumers are increasingly fickle, and the abundance of aggregators such as price comparison engines make shopping around easier than ever before. Long-term brand loyalty is much less prevalent as a result of these changes. Organisations are seeking to respond to this challenge by transforming themselves and embedding the ability to change to meet customer needs into the fabric of who they are.

It is now commonplace for people to have more modern, more frequently updated technology at home than that provided by their employer. This more technically literate and better-equipped marketplace demands new and innovative digital services.

The need for Agility in organisations in order to rapidly deliver business and technological change is now well established. Providing innovative digital services to customers is essential to respond to the challenges of:

1.   Disruption of a whole industry sector by innovative commercial models delivered by digital technologies.

2.   Reduced customer loyalty and the ease of switching to new service providers.

3.   Demand from a technologically savvy customer base that is increasingly seeking better digital experiences.

DOING MORE WITH LESS

Not only do organisations now face unprecedented pressure to rapidly change and deliver new services, they must be more efficient and save costs too. Doing more with less is a common theme across all industry sectors, and achieving it means not only being good at delivering change but also becoming more efficient at running existing products and services.

Considerable work has been done over the years on Lean thinking in manufacturing, and Agile delivery in technology. In BJSS we talk about efficiency in terms of lightweight processes supporting the 'Necessary and sufficient' tasks for predictable and efficient delivery.

A DESIRE FOR PREDICTABILITY

A desire for predictability in project and technology delivery is common to all our conversations with clients. Organisations are driven to plan and budget in annual cycles, often as a result of the need to meet short-term shareholder or stakeholder expectations. Corporate governance often drives risk avoidance behaviours that are counter to the need to evolve and innovate for long term survival.

Every organisation must innovate and embrace Agility in order to survive in markets that are being disrupted with greater frequency than ever before. Innovation and Agility are the essential ingredients of a modern successful organisation, but embracing Agility cannot result in a loss of control or governance. Over many years we have adapted Agile techniques to harness the benefits of incremental delivery and the flexibility to change whilst providing a degree of predictability and linkage to good governance practices.

The key to predictability is not to try and know everything upfront before committing to something, but to know just enough that the risk profile is understood. Key risks can then be managed and surprises during delivery avoided. This requires properly configured and experienced teams, supported by sufficient, lightweight processes.

A BRIEF OVERVIEW OF AGILE

Agile ways of working have existed in software development since the Agile manifesto was first conceived in 2001. The focus of the Agile manifesto is to free teams from excessive process, plans and documents and instead work closely with the user to deliver working software. In order to innovate and deliver rapid change it makes sense to adopt Agile principles across the organisation.

A common misconception is that Agile supports extremes of behaviour, for example not documenting software. This is incorrect. Rather than mandating an extreme position, the Agile manifesto shown in **Figure 1-1** simply expresses a bias for the items on the left of each value over the items on the right.

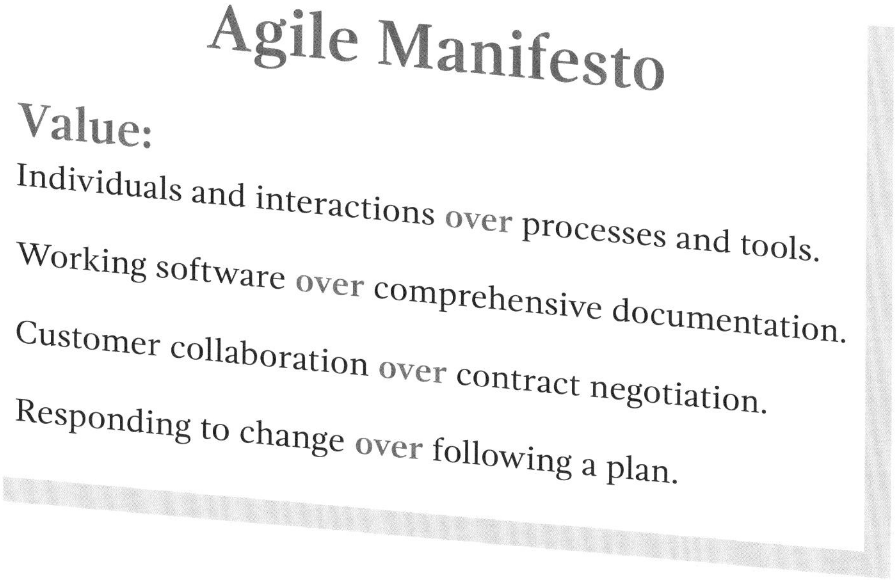

Agile Manifesto

Value:

Individuals and interactions over processes and tools.

Working software over comprehensive documentation.

Customer collaboration over contract negotiation.

Responding to change over following a plan.

Figure 1-1 : The Agile Manifesto

Another challenge is that many people think Agile is itself a process and that to become Agile involves implementing a methodology. This misses the point. Agility is about a way of being that guides behaviours. Agile is something you **are** not something you **do**.

Many of the tenets of the Agile manifesto can also apply to the wider organisation. The important point is to recognise real-world constraints and to retain 'Necessary and sufficient' governance.

BJSS OPINION

THE VALUE TRIANGLE

In previous editions of this book we discussed the concept of the iron triangle for a software development project. This considers the triple constraint of scope, time and cost and the challenge of meeting all three simultaneously to create a quality outcome.

This update addresses a broader triple constraint facing organisations, particularly the technology function - the Value Triangle. This challenges CIOs to deliver technology predictably, with low risk whilst retaining organisational flexibility and Agility, at the same time as reducing costs and delivering value for money.

This updated Value Triangle is shown in **Figure 1-2** and is something we address throughout this book.

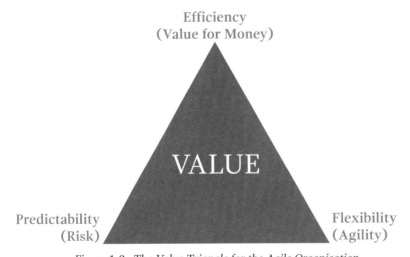

Figure 1-2 : The Value Triangle for the Agile Organisation

BECOMING A MORE AGILE ORGANISATION

Organisations must become more Agile - to embrace change, innovate and be more responsive to user needs.

This book offers practical insights into organisation, processes, and techniques to deliver change and technology-led products. It is worth noting that becoming a more Agile organisation is an on-going journey – not a one-off activity and so we do not offer a prescriptive target operating model for the organisation.

Embracing change requires good working practices, with feedback loops for continuous improvement, and a supportive culture and values system for the people involved. Organisations that combine these essential ingredients will thrive.

CHANGE OFTEN

Becoming a flexible organisation involves becoming comfortable with change as a routine activity. This is good for the organisation as it enables it to be responsive to customer needs and more readily realise value from those relationships.

Change can be unsettling for the people involved, but we believe it is worth pushing through this and using a culture and values system to support individuals in feeling secure in an organisation that regularly innovates and adapts.

Another barrier to frequent change is often an aversion to the 'risk' of technology change. This generally becomes a self-fulfilling prophecy. Due to the perceived risk of technology changes, rigorous approval gates and associated process overhead are mandated in an attempt to reduce the risk of failure. This high 'release tax' ensures change is less frequent and, as a consequence, more changes are put into each release. Bigger changes of course carry a greater risk of failure. Modern DevOps and Continuous Delivery techniques can help break this cycle.

OVERCOMING POTENTIAL BARRIERS TO AGILITY

Moving towards a more Agile organisation, able to rapidly embrace change, isn't without challenges, but the benefits are worthwhile. Recent innovations in technology and delivery approaches have provided mechanisms for surmounting many of the traditional barriers to organisational Agility. Throughout this book we offer some insights into how to overcome some of the typical challenges outlined in **Table 1-1**.

Barrier	Enabler	Benefit
Insufficient insight and information into user needs.	Fast feedback from frequent release cycles and community input from social media.	Increased flexibility to meet customer needs.
Lack of understanding of Agile methods and principles across the organisation.	Increased pervasiveness of Agile and a variety of maturing methods. Read this book!	Improved culture of delivery and customer focus. Teams bound by common goals, enhanced employee engagement.
Resistance to change and attachment to existing organisational boundaries.	Greater autonomy and empowerment for Agile teams and individuals.	Opportunity for employees to have greater visibility of the value added by their contribution.
Existing supplier contracts and incentives not aligned to broader goals.	Agile contracting based on outcomes and organisational goals.	Suppliers can contribute more directly to the overall value delivered.
Imperative to maximise existing investments in physical technology.	Flexible on-demand infrastructure provisioning using Cloud technology.	Can leverage more flexible commercial models and reduce capital investment.
Procurement and compliance processes limiting flexibility to introducing technology.	Open Source technologies that can be downloaded and used immediately.	Lower procurement and technology costs and teams can start delivering sooner.
Risk-averse culture and high overhead for technology releases and business change.	Smaller, more frequent releases of changes that are inherently less risky.	Greater flexibility to respond to evolving market needs.
Funding and governance models geared towards big decisions rather than several smaller ones.	Value-based investment decisions made more often for smaller amounts by empowered teams.	Can 'fail fast' and learn with minimal investment.

Table 1-1 : Challenges and Benefits of Organisation Agility

The Enterprise Agile Approach

Built on Experience

As a supplier that values long term client relationships and organic growth, we recognise the importance of delivering on our commitments. In order to do this, we have developed the approach described in this book. BJSS Enterprise Agile is what we believe 'Good looks like' in terms of implementing technology change and running technology services. The ideas, processes and philosophy outlined here are embodied in the work we do in order for us to be successful as a supplier and for our clients to realise the value of their investment.

A focus on delivery is embedded in our psyche. Many evangelists theorise about how to deliver change and technology initiatives. We have written this book based on practical experience and insights and lessons learned from delivering hundreds of projects over more than twenty years, to a broad range of clients in sectors as diverse as Government, Media, Retail and Financial Services.

This perspective is an important dimension that is often missed from other texts on Agility. If your vendor model is not aligned to enterprise architecture and the delivery model, significant issues are likely. Organisational tensions and politics arising from misaligned goals will adversely impact the delivery of effective change.

Most organisations of any scale work with multiple suppliers to deliver all or part of their operational business processes, customer engagement and technology. It is only when supplier incentives and vendor management are consistent with the organisational goals, architecture and delivery model, that true Agility is possible.

Founding Principles

Successfully delivering change is first and foremost about people. Whatever the change initiative, the outcome will be determined by bringing people on the journey and engaging high-ability teams to deliver.

Supporting the teams delivering services are the lightweight patterns, processes, technology and tooling that we describe.

In order to guide any change initiative we focus closely on two key components:

Insight - into the needs of the user and the marketplace.

High Quality Engineering - to underpin and de-risk the delivery.

Ultimately the goal of any change initiative is to create value for the organisation. Delivering business and technological change must be guided by insight and sound engineering discipline. Supporting this are a number of essential principles:

1. **Risk-First** - prioritising change based on risk profile.

2. **Architecture-centric** – quality engineering built on strong architecture.

3. **Quality Built-in** – embedding quality from the outset.

4. **Transparency** – clarity throughout the delivery process.

5. **Innovation** – thinking beyond the usual solution.

6. **Necessary and Sufficient** – doing just enough of the right things.

WHERE TO GO NEXT

This book recommends good practice in the areas of People, Process and Technology - the three ingredients required for organisational Agility. If you are new to some of the concepts here you may wish to read from start to finish. Readers looking to pursue specific topics might want to choose from those listed below.

Within each chapter we provide a consistent structure that introduces key concepts, offers our opinion and experience and outlines the BJSS Enterprise Agile method for achieving success.

CHAPTER 2 – THE JOURNEY TO AGILITY

Introduces some of the principles important in achieving greater Agility in both organisations and product delivery whilst managing risk.

CHAPTER 3 - A PATTERN FOR DELIVERING VALUE

Provides a map of the approaches to delivering products to customers and introduces the BJSS Enterprise Agile product lifecycle.

CHAPTER 4 - THE OPTIMAL TEAM

Discusses how to structure people around the process and the human factors to be considered in creating productive teams.

CHAPTER 5 - EFFECTIVE LEADERSHIP

Identifies the leadership skills and practices essential to building and running quality products.

CHAPTER 6 - ANALYSING USER NEEDS

Outlines a structured approach to capturing user needs and focusing on achieving organisation outcomes.

CHAPTER 7 - CRAFTING THE PRODUCT INCREMENT

Describes the anatomy of the Sprint as the unit of delivery and the daily operating rhythm of delivery teams.

Chapter 8 - Engineering Quality Outcomes

Explores the delivery pipeline and engineering practices used in changing and running products to a high standard.

Chapter 9 - Service Agility

Describes how Enterprise Agile combines traditional structured Service Management approaches with Agile delivery.

Chapter 10 - Making it Work

Suggests where to start with implementing greater Agility in the organisation and making it work in a client and supplier relationship.

Chapter 11 - Afterword

Provides a link to more practical details of how to implement BJSS Enterprise Agile in your organisation.

Appendix A - Engineering Successful Change

Presents some 'Golden rules' for achieving a 'No surprises end-game'.

Appendix B - Glossary

Defines some of the key terms used throughout the book.

KEY POINTS

1 Rapid change is essential if organisations are to survive disruption by digital transformation.

2 Organisations are looking to create value through change and are grappling with the triple constraint of flexibility, efficiency and predictability.

3 Many of the historic barriers to greater Agility have been dissolved by new approaches and technologies.

4 The BJSS Enterprise Agile approach focuses on insight into user needs and high quality engineering principles.

5 This book describes a method for building and running technology-led products based on over 20 years' practical experience.

2

The Journey to Agility

Organisations are seeking greater Agility in order to thrive in the digital economy. Meeting this challenge requires updated thinking on how to build and run technology and how to weave this new approach into the organisational fabric.

Greater Agility requires a combination of the right people, supported by the organisational culture and values, lightweight processes and appropriate tools. We start by exploring some of these key components and the essential things that enable Agility.

CONCEPTS

TECHNOLOGY AT THE HEART OF THE ORGANISATION

Organisations have historically imposed functional divides within their internal structure. There is of course a need to group people and processes in an organisation of any reasonable scale. The challenge as organisations grow is that people can develop an affinity to their job function at the expense of the delivery of business value through the product or service they provide.

Enabling true organisation-wide Agility requires a rethink of what organisations look and feel like. The established view of IT as an internal service provider, separate from 'the business' requires re-examination. Technology can no longer be seen as merely useful tools provided by the IT department to assist the business execute its processes. To deliver innovative digital services, all modern organisations need technology at their core. In fact, the successful modern organisation is fundamentally a technology organisation operating in a particular domain.

Figure 2-1 : Organisational Convergence

CIOs now more than ever need to understand how technology can add value to the organisation while CMOs need to understand what it can offer customers. In a rush to meet these challenges many organisations have appointed a CDO (Chief Digital Officer). This move may help to get to a digital strategy more quickly, but to be able to transform into a truly Agile organisation that can rapidly deliver change, a deeper cultural and structural change is required.

We explore culture and organisation in more detail in Chapter 4.

MULTI-SPEED IT

Delivering new and innovative digital services will not typically be a green-field adventure. Unless you are a start-up or relatively young organisation you will already have mature back office systems, legacy technology and a wealth of experience around your customer needs and business processes. The challenge is to leverage existing knowledge and systems to change rapidly - without being constrained by a lack of elasticity in the legacy world.

Many have already considered this dilemma and produced a variety of models to allow for varying rates of change. Much of this thinking is based on the concept of Shearing Layers - the different refresh rates of the components of a building: 'Site, Structure, Skin, Services, Space and Stuff'. The site on which a building is placed is fixed forever. The structure of a building is expected to last tens of years, whilst the services, layout and décor will change more frequently.

The use of Shearing Layers is adopted by the architectural principle of Pace Layering that designs buildings with future adaptability in mind.

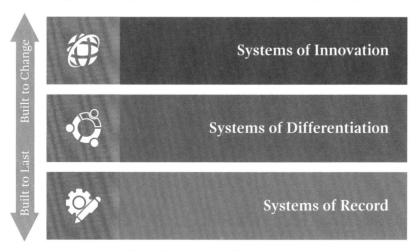

Figure 2-2 : Gartner Pace Layering

Pace Layering was introduced into the technology domain by Gartner. Within the technology model it is acknowledged that different systems can evolve at different speeds based on their proximity to the end customer and the need for innovation.

The idea of multi-speed technology change was also popularised by Geoffrey Moore, who proposed that rapidly changing Systems of

Engagement could be used to fuel innovation and develop new services with more stable Systems of Record as foundations.

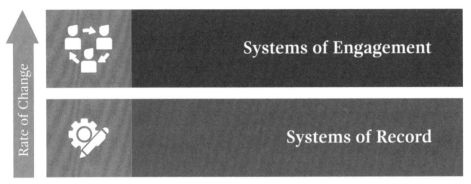

Figure 2-3 : Bi-modal Technology Change

These models can be thought of as multi-lane highways with a different velocity of change delivered in each lane. Both models highlight two key points that we will return to a number of times throughout this book:

1. There is no 'One size fits all' delivery approach.

2. Strong architecture is essential.

The point on architecture is important - it is why being 'Architecture-centric' is a core value of Enterprise Agile. You can only achieve this proposed separation of layers if your technology stack supports it. This is where well defined APIs and service layers become essential. It also blows away the notion of an emergent architecture for any appreciable change initiative - a fatal flaw in many Agile deliveries.

THE PRODUCT PORTFOLIO

The concept of portfolio management dates back to the 1970s. Whereas Projects and Programmes are temporary structures that deliver change, a portfolio is an enduring model of the applications in the organisation and is used to direct investment.

Figure 2-4 shows an early method of categorising the portfolio devised by McFarlan. This matrix provides four basic classifications of application.

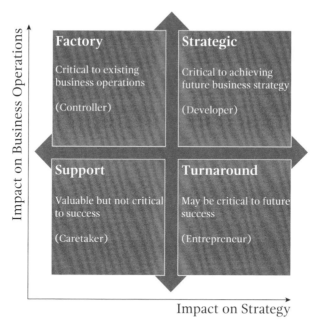

Figure 2-4 : McFarlan's Portfolio Matrix

Complementing a portfolio view of applications is the ITIL (Information Technology Infrastructure Library) service portfolio or catalogue. Similarly, this describes the services provided by a technology function often related to the support of the application portfolio. Within the modern organisation a portfolio management approach is still relevant, although separation of applications and services is likely to be replaced by a common view of the technology-led products provided to internal and external user communities.

INNOVATION AS A CATALYST FOR AGILITY

All organisations are looking to change at an increasing pace to meet the Agility challenge set out in Chapter 1. Whilst start-ups have a perceived advantage over established organisations with significant legacy technology and processes, this need not necessarily be the case. Whilst it is also true that being small can make change easier, the key factor is not size, or being new - it is **innovation**.

Many established organisations can find it hard to innovate, having spent considerable time and effort optimising their organisations for operational efficiency. This optimisation does not create an environment, nor encourage the behaviours required for innovation. Nobody could argue against the need for innovation - just look at the fall of Blockbuster and the rise of Netflix, or the decline of Blackberry as a dominant force in the mobile phone market and the success of Apple and the iPhone.

What is innovation, and how can all organisations embrace it?

Some organisations embrace the concept of Innovation Labs to generate new ideas for products and services, whilst for some this is built into the fabric of the firm. However innovation is achieved, it is important to have a process, the right behaviours and lean thinking.

One model that describes the characteristics of innovation is the Harvard Definition of the Innovators DNA as illustrated in **Figure 2-5**. Adopting these behaviours is an essential part of making innovation work in any organisation.

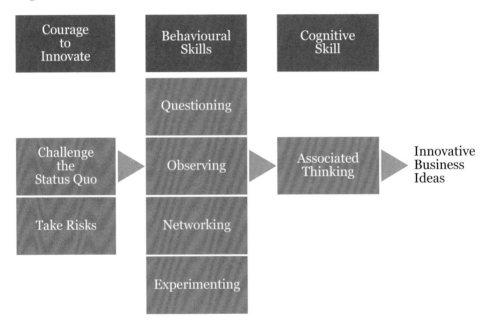

Figure 2-5 : Harvard Definition of the Innovator's DNA

TAKING A PRODUCT OR PROJECT PERSPECTIVE

How an organisation delivers change is largely driven by the perspective of the products provided. Where 'Run' the organisation and 'Change' the organisation are distinct activities, full organisational Agility cannot be achieved. In this traditional model the vehicle for delivering change is the project. Some organisations are able to take a product perspective and see both operating and enhancing a product as 'Business as Usual' activities. Within this model the capacity of the product team dictates the speed at which change is delivered.

Key to whether an organisation takes a product or project perspective is often governance and funding. Run activities are typically funded from operational expenditure, while Change is usually a capital investment.

Using Projects and Programmes as a container for change is not necessarily a bad thing. It can be useful for getting to an initial product launch, for example. However, there are significant benefits to breaking down barriers between 'Change' and 'Run' teams and having a combined retained product team.

The most obvious downside to projects is that they are temporary structures. Considerable energy is required to form a team that becomes a productive coherent unit. Organisations should start thinking about change as business as usual rather than a discrete project activity.

BJSS OPINION

THE HIERARCHY OF CONCERNS

In order to build a model of what 'Good' looks like, it is useful to dimension the solution space in a number of ways. A good starting point is to consider the hierarchy of responsibilities and activities in product delivery. Progressing through successive levels reveals further detail and a lower level of granularity.

Organisation
- Strategy and Organisation Roadmap
- Culture and Values
- Sourcing and Supplier Strategy
- Enterprise Architecture
- Governance and Finance

Portfolio
- Prioritising initiatives to deliver strategy
- Integration and management of dependencies
- Allocation of resources
- Business Architecture
- Value-based investment decisions

Product
- Product Roadmap
- Product Backlog & Direction
- Release Planning & Prioritisation
- User Communication and Feedback
- Solution Architecture
- Service Metrics

Delivery
- Delivery Backlog
- Detailed Estimation
- Work Allocation
- User-centric Design
- Technical Assurance
- Delivery Metrics

Figure 2-6 : Hierarchy of Concerns

Figure 2-6 identifies four key layers: the organisation, the portfolio, the product and the delivery team. Our model is constructed on the premise that organisations operate one or more portfolios of products they wish to build upon. The focus at the organisation level is on strategy, funding and governance.

Beneath the organisation layer sits the portfolio(s) that contain the individual products that serve users and customers. Each of these products is typically technology-enabled and require focused leadership to ensure they operate and change in a way that delivers value to the organisation.

Finally, the lowest layer deals with the day-to-day work of the delivery team and the implementation and support of technology and business change.

ORGANISATION-LEVEL ACTIVITIES

The organisation needs to layout the context and framework within which product teams can deliver value. Ultimately the organisation needs to establish a strategy and set goals and a roadmap. This process will be most effective when there is a feedback loop. This insight will come from product teams and will always be guided by information relating to the success of current products, user needs and general movement in the market.

A complete discussion of business strategy and marketing is beyond the scope of this book. It is important to reflect on the attributes of strategy and organisational level constraints that influence the work of product teams in delivering change and operating effectively.

STRATEGY AND ROADMAP

We expect there to be a forward vision for the direction of the organisation and its implications for the products and services offered. The organisation's strategy will address the markets it is targeting, and the range of products and services on offer.

Product teams should be empowered to deliver against this strategy by maximising value through evolving their product to meet ever-changing user needs. A broad roadmap for the organisation should highlight the introduction of new products into the portfolio or the retirement and replacement of legacy ones.

CULTURE AND VALUES

The organisation's culture and values should support the work of the product teams. The tone and behaviours of the team and its ability to collaborate effectively towards delivery should be reinforced by the organisation. Every organisation has a different focus, and this plays an important part in guiding product teams.

A challenge we often see is when multiple suppliers are engaged in support of a product team, or parts of the organisation are outsourced. Ideally you would want all suppliers collaborating towards the common goal of delivering the most advantageous change for the organisation. This requires not only the correct sourcing strategy but we also recommend that all supplier staff are properly introduced to the culture and values of the host organisation.

SOURCING AND SUPPLIER STRATEGY

The approach taken to the use of suppliers by an organisation and the strategy for the use of internal and external resources plays a pivotal role in the success of any product. We believe that good delivery is ability-led and relies on having strong people in key roles. The procurement and utilisation of the right resource for the job is a critical success factor.

All too often procurement functions have been given objectives by the organisation that do not align to the objectives of the product teams. Ultimately all functions in the organisation should be focused on the common goal of adding value. Collaboration and effective working across the supply chain are key to Agility and a balance is required such that the commercial interests of all parties are preserved.

Where a product team wishes to make use of external products or services, it is recommended that support from procurement or vendor management is embedded within the team. Increasing organisational Agility should not mean giving free reign to suppliers. By including the vendor management function within the product team, supplier performance management can be more relevant within the context of the work being undertaken.

ENTERPRISE ARCHITECTURE

In an organisation of any reasonable scale we expect to see some form of Enterprise Architecture function. This group needs to provide a clear set of lightweight constraints and guidance within which product teams can operate and deliver change. There is a clear balance to be struck. We are not in favour of ivory towers and overly prescriptive corporate standards that get in the way of Agility.

The Enterprise Architecture function operates best as a two-way dialogue and as a group that coaches and supports product teams, rather than simply passing down standards. The key reason for this function is to help the organisation move forward at pace rather than hold it back. To this end, Enterprise Architecture should primarily be about providing guidance. This will enable the experience from past lessons learned to benefit the team, rather than simply enforcing standards.

Certain strategic goals in the organisation may require support from the Enterprise Architecture function. It may be necessary, for example, to re-platform technology to introduce new levels of interoperability across a range of products. This type of broader organisation initiative will require overarching architectural support.

Several Enterprise Architecture models exist and their coverage is beyond the scope of this book. It is useful to draw attention to the core elements that we expect the function to cover. The four key components are: Business Architecture, Information Architecture, Application Architecture and Technology Architecture as shown in **Figure 2-7**.

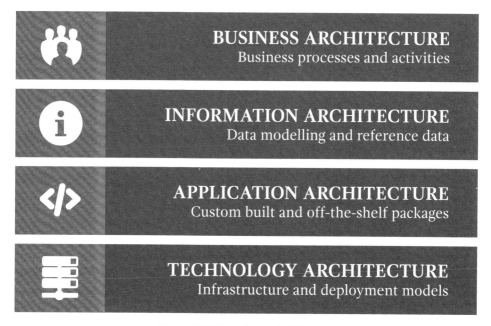

Figure 2-7 : Four Layer Architecture

The Enterprise Architecture function will only cover the lightweight standards around these areas. Most of the specific detail will come from the solution architecture for specific products.

GOVERNANCE AND FUNDING

Resources in terms of people and finance will be allocated across the portfolio of products by the organisation. The level of dynamism in this process will determine the level of Agility the organisation can achieve. Funding will normally be allocated through an annual planning process and corresponds to a related need to report financial results to shareholders. This is often a real-world constraint that cannot be changed.

Through an appropriate governance process it is possible that funding across the portfolio may be allocated more dynamically, however this is unlikely to work for large-scale capital investment projects. A common route to funding change is allocating a budget to individual products. This effectively sets a resource capacity that Product Owners are empowered to use as they see fit to maximise value for the organisation.

A lightweight but effective governance process should sit between the broader organisation and the Product Teams. Governance should effectively draw together stakeholders from Architecture, Delivery Management and Product Ownership to ensure proper alignment and decision making. Where relevant, it is likely that vendor management or suppliers would also be represented. We cover governance in more detail in Chapter 5.

MAPPING THE PORTFOLIO

The system landscape in many organisations is often quite complex. Mapping the portfolio can be undertaken in a number of ways depending on the view required. The decision as to the appropriate approach is informed by the desired rate of change and the criticality of the system, as illustrated in **Figure 2-8**.

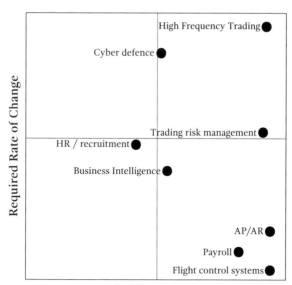

Figure 2-8 : Mapping System Changes

Mapping out the organisation's portfolio of products and services in this way can be very helpful. It allows the organisation to take a view on where investment should go and also advise as to the types of teams and suppliers to apply. **Figure 2-9** introduces some broad categories of approach.

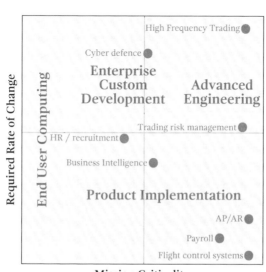

Figure 2-9 : Technical Implementation Based on System Mapping

The Enterprise Agile Approach

Components of the Technology Landscape

In our approach we recommend that modern organisations embrace a number of concepts within the technology space. The underlying culture and values of the organisation support these components and guide all behaviours and decision making.

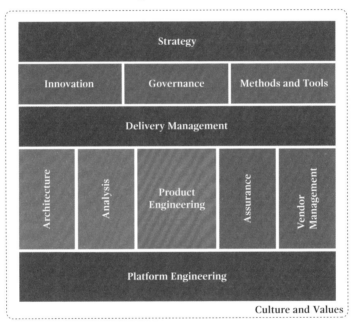

Figure 2-10 : Components of the Technology Landscape

At the core of technology delivery are the strategic and supporting functions of Innovation, Governance, and Methods and Tooling. These functions serve to determine direction and provide oversight on delivery and are often combined into the 'Office of the CIO'.

Delivering change and supporting the technology products of the organisation is the remit of product engineering teams. These teams are aligned to particular products and are principally concerned with the delivery and maintenance of software.

Platform engineering provides the underlying infrastructure on which products are run. For many organisations this will be a public or private

Cloud solution. The platform will usually be presented to Product Teams as Infrastructure as a Service (IaaS) or Platform as a Service (PaaS), allowing them to code against APIs and self-provision infrastructure, removing a traditional blocker to Agility - long infrastructure lead times.

THE INNOVATION LAB

An Innovation Lab is useful for facilitating Agility in the organisation. Some organisations may have dedicated Innovation Labs, others may spin one up for a short period of time, or bring in a third party to facilitate one for them.

Either way, the key point is that the lab has a lean process for generating innovative technology-led business ideas. Its purpose is to create a business idea that may be developed further into a product with the organisations portfolio.

An Innovation Lab functions best when 'Innovators DNA' behaviours are combined with lean thinking and a process for the generation and refinement of potential ideas. Our process for ideation is illustrated in **Figure 2-11**. The model seeks to open up the idea generation process and align with organisation goals and desired outcomes.

Figure 2-11 : The Ideation Process

KEY POINTS

1 The successful modern organisation has technology at its core as an enabler, rather than a discrete supporting function.

2 Multi-speed IT provides a useful model for introducing Agility to systems that engage customers.

3 Agility can be increased by taking a product perspective of continuous change rather than discrete projects.

4 Technology delivery is guided by the organisation's culture and values system.

5 Innovation labs are a powerful tool for creating new ideas and introducing Agility into the organisation.

3

A Pattern for Delivering Value

Our aim with this book is to highlight good practice for using Agility to introduce and enhance technology products. In the opening chapters we explored the challenges facing organisations and the rationale for our approach. In this chapter we describe the patterns and practices for delivering value.

No 'One size fits all' methodology or approach is appropriate to every change initiative. Rather, one of a number of common approaches can be adapted to suit the needs of the organisation, framed by a supportive culture and values system.

Increasing organisational Agility is a journey and is not achieved by rigidly implementing a new operating model. Success comes from embracing Agile techniques and an Agile mind-set.

CONCEPTS

THE EVOLUTION OF AGILE METHODS

What we now describe as 'Agile methods' began appearing in the early 1990s, before the Agile manifesto. These early methods focused on developing individual software applications in isolation. Born out of the frustration of working in a process-heavy environment, software engineers sought a more effective way of working closely with users to develop the software they needed.

Many of these early methods eschewed all process and were often criticised for letting software projects become 'Developer playgrounds' with insufficient formality for Enterprise-scale change initiatives. This frustration with early attempts at Agile led us to develop the BJSS Enterprise Agile approach. Our aim was to help clients enjoy the benefits of greater flexibility and efficiency, whilst retaining predictability and achieving a 'No surprises end-game' for delivery projects.

Recent developments have seen the growth of scaled Agile approaches that seek to address larger change initiatives. Whilst some of these are gaining traction, they are still largely software focused and do not always link effectively to organisation governance and business change.

XP

Extreme Programming (XP) is an early Agile methodology dating back to the late 1990s. It identifies twelve practices and several supporting activities, values and principles. Most commonly known for pair programming, XP also promoted practices such as programmer welfare through development at a sustainable pace.

Whilst not often applied in a text book fashion, some of the core elements of XP remain at the heart of Agile delivery, notably continuous integration and test-driven development. A criticism of XP is that it is best suited to small teams and does not scale effectively.

(R)UP

The Unified Process (UP) refers to the generic process that was popularised as the Rational Unified Process (RUP) after the commercial toolset of that name and to a lesser extent in the Open Source version,

Open UP. The key elements of UP are a project lifecycle comprising four phases: Inception, Elaboration, Construction and Transition.

The previous version of BJSS Enterprise Agile extended a number of UP principles including a focus on risk and architecture, with iterative and incremental delivery. The strong link between UP and the RUP toolset caused many to think it was a commercial methodology requiring the toolset and was in part a factor in its declining usage.

Scrum

Also originating in the 1990s, Scrum is what many people will recognise as a common Agile approach. Scrum provides definition of roles, events and artefacts, many of which have entered common parlance and some of which have been adopted by the BJSS Enterprise Agile approach.

Scrum has become a very popular Agile method and has proven effective, particularly on small scale initiatives. In response to the desire to take Scrum principles and apply them to larger scale problems, newer methods such as Large Scale Scrum (LeSS) have emerged.

LeSS

Large Scale Scrum (LeSS) is an attempt to identify how Scrum can be scaled effectively to bigger teams. Based on experience and thinking of using Scrum at scale it was formalised in 2005. Two variants of LeSS exist - LeSS for up to 8 teams and LeSS Huge for bigger groups. It provides a framework that covers principles, structure, management, technical excellence and adoption.

SAFe

The Scaled Agile Framework (SAFe) has been through three revisions since 2012 and through its 'Big Picture', illustrates a process for Agile delivery at scale. SAFe makes a distinction between Team, Programme and Portfolio and introduces the concept of the 'Agile Release Train'.

As a method for scaled Agile delivery SAFe has been gaining in popularity, however it has faced criticism from the Agile community for not being pure Agile and being too rigid. Some also say it lacks a strong user focus and feedback loop from the user community.

DevOps and the Convergence in Technology

In the early days of Agile software development, it was recognised that for effective delivery, the divide between different technology disciplines such as Developers and Testers needed to be broken down. Multi-disciplinary teams focused on the common goal of delivering working software rather than throwing work 'over the wall'. More recently, DevOps practices have advocated bringing together Development and Technical Operations as a single team responsible for the traditionally separate activities of building and running a software system. We address this topic in more detail in Chapter 8.

Figure 3-1 : Convergence Within Technology Departments

This convergence is key to achieving savings in the operational side of the organisation.

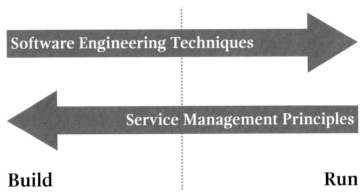

Figure 3-2 : Transfer of Methods in DevOps

As shown in **Figure 3-2** the adoption of DevOps techniques allows cohesive teams to efficiently build and run products for their customers.

Software engineering techniques and automation have moved over the line from project delivery into Operations, while service management techniques have moved back into Development. It is the automation of many error-prone manual processes that reduces the barrier to rapid change and takes much of the effort out of operating a technology product.

Continuous Delivery

Regardless of the mechanism for getting change into the hands of users, during delivery we would always want to divide change into bite-sized pieces. At the end of each piece, the team reviews where they are and solicits feedback. Typically this means working within time boxed periods known as 'Iterations' or 'Sprints' which bound a discrete set of changes to be delivered. After one or more Sprints, the changes are released to the user. This forms the basis of incremental delivery.

It is also possible that changes are immediately released to the user independent of each other. This model offers greater flexibility and is often better suited to small scale change and relatively mature products.

Continuous delivery is a method of fully automating software production, quality assurance and deployment using a delivery pipeline through which software change can flow, enabling deployment into production at any time. Irrespective of the overarching delivery pattern adopted, continuous delivery and the use of repeatable automated processes is powerful and forms a key part of the BJSS Enterprise Agile approach.

Cloud

It is worth calling out Cloud as a key enabler to Agility and facet of the delivery pattern. Agile methods have historically focused on the production of software. Treatment of infrastructure delivery is often scant or non-existent. Traditional 'tin and wires' infrastructure provisioning led to project plan dependencies rather than Agile ways of working.

With Cloud, or more specifically Software Defined Infrastructure, increments of change to products can include not only the application software but the corresponding changes to the infrastructure too, packaged and released simultaneously. This opens up a powerful new paradigm in systems delivery and enables new architectures based on lightweight micro-services to be easily deployed.

Different Change Scenarios

In defining our thinking around delivering change we have explored several common scenarios that we see regularly and have considerable experience of. Organisations must address a huge variety of change initiatives, but we feel these scenarios cover the bulk of the cases. Frequently occurring initiatives in Business to Business (B2B), Business to Consumer (B2C) or Government to Citizen (G2C) include:

Web Scale Platform Evolution

Large modern technology organisations often embrace Agility at scale. Where they have a single product and no significant legacy, they are able to apply Agile methods across the organisation and release change often. Examples include companies such as Facebook, Spotify, etc.

Change Programmes

Often requiring significant capital investment and business change these programmes typically arise as a result of mergers and acquisition, the need for a platform refresh or the expiration of outsourcing agreements. The scale of the change, funding model and often big bang nature of cutover impacts the level of Agility achieved.

Enhancement Projects

Most organisations run projects continuously to enhance the technology products within their portfolio. It would be possible to write a whole book on the philosophical point of '*Is there such a thing as an Agile project?*' Greater Agility is clearly achieved by releasing often and making value-based decisions on delivery priorities. This can be at odds with traditional project funding processes which require an agreed business case upfront.

Greenfield Project

Creating a new relatively standalone product can be undertaken in quite an Agile manner. Feature priorities are addressed based on user need and business value to create a Minimum Viable Product (MVP).

PROOF OF CONCEPTS

Small scale PoC work is a prime candidate for lean working methods and Agility. With this type of work a fast feedback loop is a powerful tool to direct the effort of the team towards the objectives.

AGILITY IN ALL SCENARIOS

The challenge is how to obtain the benefits of Agility across the full range of change initiatives. It is easy to see why small scale changes are a good candidate for Agile delivery, particularly on mature products. The adoption of Agility in larger solutions tends to be in organisations that have adopted a *product*, rather than *project*, perspective and have placed technology at the heart of the organisation.

Agility is often lost on large scale change programmes, where several factors impact the level of Agility:

1. **Funding** – Change programmes typically involve a large capital investment that requires a detailed upfront business case and scoping exercise.

2. **Delivery Model** – It can be difficult to deliver change in small pieces, particularly on large programmes that might, for example, be replacing a legacy product.

3. **Vendor Model** – Where several suppliers are engaged it is easy to create silos that create barriers to Agility.

4. **Architecture** – Strong architecture is required to enable delivery on large programmes to be decomposed effectively.

Within this book and the BJSS Enterprise Agile method, we describe techniques to enable Agile ways of working in all of these scenarios.

BJSS Opinion

Releasing Change to the Users

Earlier we discussed different types of change initiative and how these might be delivered through continuous product innovation or discrete projects. Ideally we want to break down large changes into smaller manageable chunks and put them in front of real users to get feedback. Piecemeal introduction of change allows for regular course corrections. These subtle direction changes keep the product aligned with the market and optimise the value derived by the organisation.

The constructs used will depend on two key factors:

1. How the organisation allocates funding and measures value delivered.

2. The process by which change can be delivered to the user.

There are situations when frequent releases are not possible, for example replacing a legacy trading system - all users need all functionality and all have to be in the same market - a big bang transition is unavoidable.

Ideally you would want to release change to users often and as small incremental features, because:

1. The users benefit from new product features.

2. The organisation gains value.

3. The Product Team receives feedback to refine the roadmap.

4. Change becomes a low risk 'Business as Usual' activity.

There are of course many real-world constraints and differences across sectors and products. Continuously delivering change to a social media networking application is likely to be easier than to a commodities trading platform, for example.

It is worth spending some time exploring the factors that impact release cycles. Firstly let's tackle a key challenge for many organisations – perceived risk. We purposefully use the term 'perceived risk'. It is often a very subjective assessment based on prior experience that may or may not be relevant. Many organisations unintentionally develop a risk-averse culture, perhaps based on the reaction to a previous failed release.

Attitude to risk often leads to a self-fulfilling prophecy. Change is perceived as risky, this results in additional process and a high 'release tax'. As a result, changes are made less often and releases become bigger, and as a result more risky. The automation and DevOps techniques we talk about in this book are key to breaking out of this cycle.

A further important determinant of the change cycle is impact on the user and other product and services. Where a change involves new ways of working, new people in new roles and so forth, then more up-front planning is required. These non-Agile real world constraints, such as recruitment and training, get in the way of continuous change. Again this is a good argument for changing regularly and in small chunks.

Another category of impact concerns integration with other technology products, some which may reside outside of the organisation. In these circumstances changes have to be aligned with change in other upstream or downstream systems. This is why strong architecture is so crucial to achieving Agility. Good enterprise architecture will enable integration across systems changing at different speeds.

WHEN LARGE SCALE CHANGE IS UNAVOIDABLE

Releasing changes to existing products often comes down to attitude to risk and an assessment of the impact or scale of the change. One common class of problem is worth exploring further.

Launching a new product involves a large change, particularly if replacing a legacy system. This situation is often unavoidable, for example re-writing an outsourced service that is coming to end of contract.

The new product must reach critical mass for it to be useful - this feature set is often referred to as the Minimum Viable Product (MVP). There are two transition options - big bang or incremental. With a big bang approach all users begin to use the product at the same time rather than it being introduced in phases.

The obvious choice is to avoid big bang due to the risk. However that is not without challenge, particularly if modifications are required to the existing system in order to run old and new in parallel. Sometimes big bang is the only option, for example when users cannot be partitioned in any way, such as on a trading platform where a single market with counterparty credit relationships exists. Big bang and incremental rollout are contrasted in **Table 3-1**.

Big Bang	Incremental
All users begin using the product at same time.	Users phased onto new product a group at a time.
Potential high risk if issue found post-launch.	Allows for feedback and refinement if issues found.
Upfront dry run tests to mitigate transition risk.	Potentially complex to plan and execute, with lengthy cutover period.
Requires long test phases to mature product.	Additional expense of parallel running with legacy system.
It is clear which system is in use.	Needs clarity over which product is system of record.

Table 3-1 : Comparing Big Bang and Incremental Transition

We have successfully transitioned systems using both big bang and incremental approaches - this is only possible by using the engineering and delivery practices highlighted later in this book.

STAYING OUT OF TROUBLE

Having reviewed and recovered many projects we have identified several common pitfalls experienced by organisations delivering technology-enabled products as listed in **Table 3-2**.

Challenge	Remedy
Failure to gain sufficient momentum due to lack of clarity and direction.	• Clearly understood and communicated goals at a macro (product) level and micro (feature) level.
	• Visible and active supporting organisation culture and values to guide team decision making.
Poor results in terms of quality and progress due to lack of motivated or suitably skilled team.	• Recognition that process is no substitute for ability, appropriate use of specialists and generalists.
	• Empowered teams and individuals working towards clear goals.

Challenge	Remedy
Persistent problems due to lack of alignment of delivery and governance models.	• For large scale changes use a phased delivery pattern and link this to key governance decisions. • Implement lightweight assurance including regular board and design authority meetings.
Inability to really know the position of delivery due to poor information.	• Clear set of metrics and KPIs around delivery to cover progress and quality against expected objectives and trends. • Use appropriate tooling to gather data at source and avoid building an industry around reporting.
Lack of suitable controls due to dogmatic approach to Agile working.	• Build communities to share experiences and ensure action is taken on feedback within and outside of the product team. • Develop lightweight metrics and assurance and maintain focus on broader organisation goals and governance.
Insufficient quality in delivered solution due to poor analysis and engineering.	• Quality built-in upfront using Agile test techniques rather than trying to add later through quality control. • Structured analysis techniques to produce quality requirements with traceability and acceptance criteria.

Table 3-2 : Common Delivery Challenges

Remember that no one approach, method or target-operating model addresses all scenarios. Delivering technology and business change is difficult. The important thing is to consider each scenario and product within the context of the organisation. Unless you are a technology start-up, you rarely get the opportunity to work in a legacy-free environment without the corresponding constraints that imposes.

THE ENTERPRISE AGILE APPROACH

A LIFECYCLE FOR PRODUCTS

We have covered the role of the organisation in operating and changing products. Any organisation will deliver a range of products and services to its customers. Whilst there is some variation, most products follow a similar path in terms of their lifecycle. The BJSS Enterprise Agile product lifecycle is illustrated in **Figure 3-3**.

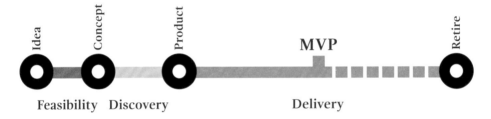

Figure 3-3 : The Product Lifecycle

Technology delivery has historically been split into 'Build' and 'Run'. Our model can, if required, support Projects and Programmes delivering change, with operation of the resultant product undertaken by technology operations and BAU teams. Our preference however, is for combined product teams undertaking Build and Run activities.

Rather than immediately focusing on these structures it is worth taking a step back and looking more holistically at the product lifecycle.

All products require some upfront work to get them to a state where there are sufficiently defined to start building and then have sufficient substance to rollout to some or all users. This is the MVP.

Once the initial version of the product is launched it will continue to evolve to meet growing user needs. These post-launch changes may be small features delivered continuously or larger features delivered incrementally by a larger change project.

Eventually the product will be retired. This process can be gradual where users are slowly migrated to a replacement product and all or part of the original product remains. It can also be a more abrupt transition when existing services are turned off. This can happen when an outsourced contract comes to an end.

Within the product lifecycle are a number of discrete phases. The early phases prepare the organisation and team for the introduction of a new product. A key focus in these early stages is to set a course and reduce risk whilst retaining Agility. Use of these phases allows the organisation to make investment decisions and informed choices about delivery options, for example to build or buy technology components.

The three phases of Feasibility, Discovery and Delivery act as a '**ready, aim, fire**' mechanism to prepare the organisation for the commitment of developing a new product. Each of these phases has a number of core objectives and should link to a governance process.

FEASIBILITY

The purpose of the Feasibility phase is to assess how an idea can meet the needs of the user and generate value for the organisation. This phase takes an idea and translates it into a more concrete concept that can be further explored.

At this stage a small team of specialists will work for a short period to determine if the idea is sufficiently substantive to warrant further effort.

DISCOVERY

The aim of a Discovery phase is to de-risk subsequent delivery and to home in on the options for implementation. Discovery will not answer all questions or establish all requirements in detail, but it will establish the scope for a MVP.

A nucleus of a product team will be formed to undertake Discovery, lasting a few weeks and delivering prototypes or product mock-ups.

DELIVERY

During the Delivery phase features of the product are incrementally delivered based on a roadmap that captures the value released to the organisation. Beyond launch the Delivery phase supports and operates the product for the users.

A cohesive product team is required. This team may exist for some time until such point as the product is retired. In some cases discrete projects are used to get to initial MVP and make subsequent enhancements, in which case temporary project teams are formed.

The key outcomes of each lifecycle phase are summarised in **Table 3-3**.

Phase	Purpose	Outcomes
Feasibility	Understand broad scope of the change, models for delivery and feasibility.	• Initial Business Case • Candidate technology solutions • Resource & Vendor model
Discovery	Perform sufficient upfront discovery to build out estimation for MVP delivery. De-risk delivery with PoCs that prove the solution architecture.	• Team and Organisation • Solution Architecture • Assurance approach • Estimation & refined costs • Functional Catalogue • Non-Functional Requirements
Delivery	Iteratively build out the solution required to implement the change. Deliver the technical and business change to users through a regular release pattern. Run the service and support users.	• Software artefacts • Business change artefacts • Business value realised • User needs met • Solutions deployed • Support incidents resolved

Table 3-3 : Lifecycle Phase Outcomes

COMPARISON WITH THE UNIFIED PROCESS PHASES

In previous editions of this book we promoted the use of the Unified Process (UP) phases for the delivery of software projects. The early phases of UP, Inception and Elaboration act in much the same way as Feasibility and Discovery do in our product lifecycle. We had always modified UP and viewed the remaining phases Construction and Transition as parallel activities, to achieve a more Agile end-game and support incremental acceptance. **Figure 3-4** illustrates the use of UP in the previous version of BJSS Enterprise Agile.

Figure 3-4 : Modified Unified Process Phases in Previous Versions of Enterprise Agile

We have introduced the new full product lifecycle in this version of our approach to address two key shortcomings of the UP phases:

1. The full product lifecycle beyond initial delivery (MVP) is not represented.

2. Construction and Transition implies a hand-off between teams or organisations and does not promote a DevOps way of working and Continuous Delivery.

Phases in the previous and current version of BJSS Enterprise Agile are compared in **Table 3-4.**

Phase	UP Phase	Comparison
Feasibility	Inception	• Equivalent focus, takes an idea from an Innovation Lab as input
Discovery	Elaboration	• Intended to achieve the same outcome
		• Intensive risk reduction process
Delivery	Construction Transition	• Continuous delivery of change with incremental acceptance
		• Release cadence may change pre- and post-MVP
		• Covers running the product and supporting users, in addition to software delivery

Table 3-4 : Comparison of Lifecycle Phases

ACHIEVING MVP – THE 'NO SURPRISES END-GAME'

As we have already discussed, getting to MVP for many products involves implementing large scale change. It is in this scenario, where large capital investments have been made, that executives get nervous and look for evidence of predictability in delivery. It is precisely for this reason that the Feasibility-Discovery-Delivery pattern is so important as a technique to de-risk delivery.

However, this should not be confused with traditional 'predictive' lifecycles such as Waterfall. A balance between upfront and deferred discovery must be struck. Just as important as charting a course during the early phases is evidencing progress in the right direction during Delivery through a process of incremental acceptance.

Figure 3-5 illustrates how incremental acceptance is achieved by running through all facets of delivery at regular intervals and validating the content and quality of the product at each stage. There are two key parts to this acceptance, firstly that the user needs are being met (functional acceptance) and secondly that the product performs adequately and can be operated effectively (non-functional acceptance).

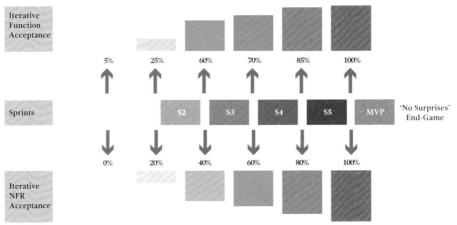

Figure 3-5 : Delivering Business Value

This process of incremental acceptance combined with the product lifecycle of BJSS Enterprise Agile are key ingredients of the 'No surprises end-game' - our delivery objective for any change initiative.

KEY POINTS

1 DevOps and Continuous Delivery techniques enable a unified delivery lifecycle to cover both change and service.

2 Where possible change should be released to users regularly and in small chunks.

3 Introducing large scale change such a replacing an existing system requires a risk-reduction pattern to get to a MVP.

4 BJSS Enterprise Agile uses Feasibility, Discovery and Delivery phases to improve predictability in implementing new initiatives.

5 Delivery should be continuous using an automated pipeline to put change into the hands of users as required and support incremental acceptance.

4

The Optimal Team

Effective delivery requires the correct organisation of highly capable people and the appropriate utilisation of their skills. Good teams are not made overnight and this is a considerable drawback of delivering change in discrete projects. Continuous delivery of change by a product team in an Agile organisation overcomes some of these challenges.

Being effective also requires that individuals and teams be supported by the culture and values of the organisation. There is a difficult balance to strike between empowering teams to make decisions and being quasi-autonomous, and potentially losing control as people operate outside the legitimate constraints put in place by the wider organisation.

CONCEPTS

THE RETURN OF THE FULL STACK ENGINEER

When BJSS was established in 1993 it was common for software engineers to perform the full range of tasks required to deliver a system. This often included not only cutting code but writing and executing automated tests, creating build and deployment scripts and maintaining development and test environments.

Over the years the software stack and the array of foundation products, frameworks and tools available to facilitate the production of a system has grown dramatically, leading many practitioners to specialise. For example larger teams often engage specialists to maintain the build servers and develop deployment scripts.

Recently the term 'Full Stack Engineer' has become popular. In our view this term describes what good all round engineers have always done - have the skill and flexibility to work on all engineering tasks required to deliver a working solution.

'Polyglot' has also recently become a fashionable term to describe a developer fluent in multiple programming languages. This too is not a new concept for us. Being skilled in several technologies can be good for the individual's career and the flexibility of the organisation, but should be balanced with a desire for in-depth knowledge in a particular field. Certainly there are cases where engineering specialism is required, for example a DBA role. We discuss what makes a good engineer later in this chapter.

It is worth saying something about another term we often hear - 'DevOps Engineer'. This role description can cause some confusion. DevOps is a cultural and organisational concept rather than a specific engineering discipline. Often what is meant is working with scripting technologies to automate the delivery pipeline. Again this is a task to which most Full Stack Engineers can turn their hand, although there are cases where a specialist can be useful. We avoid confusion by using the term Platform Engineer when referring to infrastructure delivery.

SELF-OPTIMISING ORGANISATIONS

One of the barriers to Agility we identified at the start of this book was dealing with real-world constraints and business change. Examples of potential challenges here include staff redeployment, training and recruitment. Some thinking is emerging as to how some of these issues may be overcome and how to apply Agile principles to organisation design and business change.

One such example of this is *Holacracy*, a management system devised by Brian Robertson. It replaces hierarchy and large organisational change with a flat management structure and distributed authority. Holacracy has been implemented by several hundred organisations, so while in its infancy it is gaining some ground. It demonstrates the desire amongst a variety of organisations to gain competitive advantage through a more flexible and rapidly changing structure and empowering people to take control of their own work and challenges.

BJSS OPINION

ABILITY-LED VERSUS PROCESS-LED

Successful change initiatives are ability-led not process-led. Many organisations mistakenly rely upon process to drive a quality outcome, particularly at scale. Whilst process is important, having empowered capable individuals in key roles is essential to enabling rapid change and innovation.

Commoditising or de-skilling technology delivery with excessive process is fraught with issues. We prefer to build teams from highly capable individuals with a mix of experience levels and a shared appetite for delivery success.

The Agile Manifesto reinforces this message by favouring People and Interactions over Processes and Tools. It should be noted that, as with all tenets of the Agile Manifesto this is a preferred bias rather than an extreme position. Product Teams need to operate within the constraints of the organisation and maintain a regular, healthy, connected dialogue.

Countering the perception of Agile as a 'Developer playground' requires that the organisation properly aligns teams to goals and implements the necessary and sufficient lightweight governance in preference to a return to command and control management.

A SUPPORTIVE CULTURE AND VALUES SYSTEM

Product Teams must be appropriately supported by the organisation in order to operate effectively. The organisation's culture and values exist to guide teams in their daily work, particularly when conflict arises or difficult decisions are required.

A healthy organisation will keep conversation alive through regular engagement with teams and individuals. Note that in many organisations Product Teams comprise permanent employees, contingent labour and multiple suppliers. This presents a challenge that should not be overlooked. We strongly recommend that orientation, and where necessary, adjustments to team values are made when people are added to the team.

Figure 4-1 : Aligning Individual, Team and Organisation

Ideally all individuals will contribute to, identify with, and sign up to the values of their team and the wider organisation. This simple but powerful act helps everyone move forward together. It must be clear that this is not about rigid command and control, but an evolving set of guiding principles to aid and support teams.

CREATING PRODUCTIVE TEAMS

We are often engaged in helping organisations to initiate new projects and programmes in which teams comprise people who have never worked together. This is one of the key factors why projects as a vehicle for delivering change can be inefficient. It is essential to consider, particularly in the leadership team, the characteristics of the individuals concerned and not just view each position as a role to be filled.

Various theories have been offered to describe the dynamics of a team and how a group develops. Most commonly quoted is Bruce Tuckman who initially identified four phases of group development: Forming, Storming, Norming, Performing. This was later updated to describe a fifth phase, Adjourning.

Other similar models have been proposed such as Tubbs' System Model (Orientation, Conflict, Consensus, Closure) and Fisher's theory of decision emergence (Orientation, Conflict, Emergence, Reinforcement).

These models can be useful to describe the evolution of a team and how they tackle problems. It is worth taking this into account when planning and considering the productivity of the team.

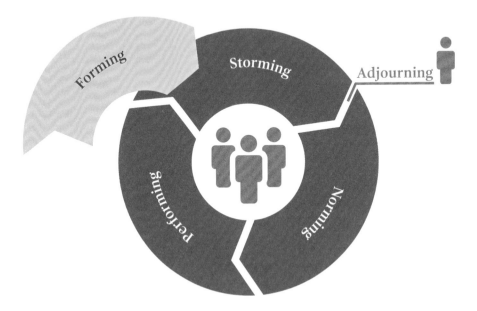

Figure 4-2 : Tuckman's Stages of Group Development

A key contributor to a productive team is clarity of goals and required outcomes. We passionately believe in keeping teams engaged and aware of the bigger picture. Team communication begins with Agile ceremonies such as the daily Stand-up, which keeps the team aligned in terms of challenges and the work of their peers.

Wider team communication should also be encouraged. This will include community gatherings for individuals interested in particular engineering disciplines, for example test automation. We also recommend that the entire product team is gathered together periodically for a full 'Town Hall' meeting. This should happen even if the team is large to re-assert objectives and allow Q&A.

Teams aren't just built in the office. Social functions are a key part of getting a team to gel and operate effectively. The leadership team can often be buried in delivery challenges and forget this essential ingredient for productivity. Assign the organisation of social functions to someone in the team - they are often likely to have better ideas and be more enthusiastic about this aspect than the management team.

CONSIDERATIONS FOR A PRODUCTIVE ENVIRONMENT

The physical environment can have a considerable impact on the ability of the team to perform. Spaces are required that support the different modes that people work in. It must be possible to work quietly and concentrate on technical tasks. In addition the environment must allow teams to collaborate and work together. This support should go beyond just traditional meeting spaces. Allowing for osmotic communication and quick informal problem solving as a team or pairing around particular problems helps keep teams productive and the work flowing.

We are often asked about the importance of co-location to delivery. Whenever possible, co-locating the whole product team is the optimal solution. As teams get larger this becomes less practical and also slightly less advantageous. Once a product team gets to around a hundred or more, people don't know each other and will not require day-to-day interactions across the broader team.

Our advice is to try and keep each delivery team together and co-located. When the overall Product Team grows to multiple delivery teams then multiple locations is an option. Working across multiple locations can be effectively supported by using appropriate communication technology and tools.

We recommend a level of lightweight formality even if teams are co-located. The use of whiteboards and cards is great for quick informal interactions and communication, however for any significant piece of work, more durable recording of work and decisions is required.

The Enterprise Agile Approach

A Brief Guide to Organisation and Teams

In order to navigate the people and organisational aspects of BJSS Enterprise Agile, a brief overview of key concepts is provided here.

First let us consider the building blocks of the delivery organisation:

1. Individuals performing specific tasks relating to change and service delivery - we promote the notion of 'T' shaped individuals.

2. Delivery and Service Teams which are highly cohesive teams of individuals working toward common goals.

3. The Product Team which consists of one or more teams and a leadership function.

These elements create a scalable method for organising people to build, maintain and enhance technology products. An effective leadership function, comprising Product Ownership, Delivery Management and Solution Architecture, is at the heart of the successful product team.

We will now explore each of these concepts in more detail.

The Product Team

The Agile organisation comprises a number of building blocks aligned to our hierarchy of concerns. Certain roles are fulfilled at an organisation level, at a product level and within engineering and business change teams. The broad picture of the Product Team and the relationships they have is shown in **Figure 4-3**.

At the heart of any Product Team are the three key roles of Solution Architecture, Delivery Management and Product Owner. These key positions decide what changes are made to the product and how the on-going service will be delivered.

This nucleus of the Product Team has the responsibility for managing the Delivery and Service teams and the relationship with user groups and stakeholders. The remainder of the Product Team is responsible for delivering change and supporting the product.

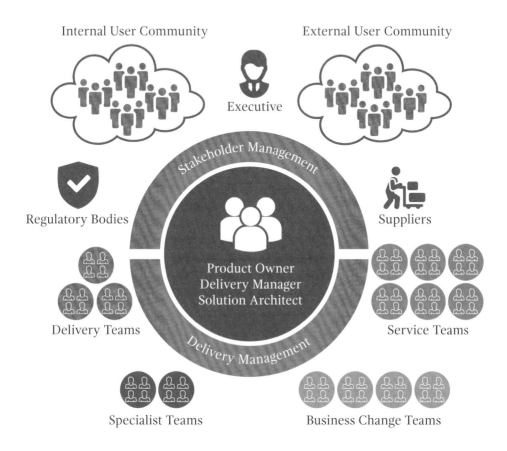

Figure 4-3 : Product Team Structure

The basic building block is the 'T' shaped technologist. These individuals are assembled into cohesive delivery teams, with potentially multiple teams for a particular product.

Most engineering teams will be multi-disciplinary and be charged with delivering end-to-end features that meet user needs and add value to the organisation. General purpose Feature delivery teams may be supported by specialist engineering teams. For example, a non-functional test team providing assurance of the complete integrated product against the non-functional requirements for the solution.

In addition to engineering teams, Service Teams will be required to deal with customer service enquiries and support the usage of the product by the organisation and external users.

In the Agile organisation there are also likely to be Business Change teams that update manual processes and execute organisational change.

THE SHAPE OF THE INDIVIDUAL

We expect teams to include a diverse range of people. The Product Team will comprise technologists, domain specialist and managers in a coherent unit organised for effective delivery. Most technologists have some kind of specialism - development, testing, analysis, database design etc. A common question is to what extent specialists should be used within technology delivery rather than generalists.

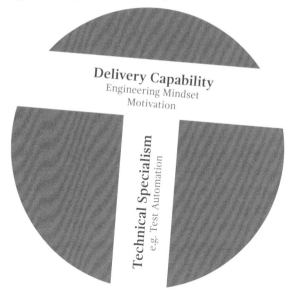

Figure 4-4 : 'T' Shaped Technologists

Achieving the benefits of Agility requires a team of people with diverse skills working together towards a common goal. However, too much specialisation risks creating silos, inefficiencies and key man dependencies that are hard to overcome.

For technology personnel we always look for 'T' shaped individuals, as illustrated in **Figure 4-4.** At their core everyone on the team has a passion for delivery, a solid understanding of Agile principles and a good engineering and problem solving mind-set. This core is supported by specialist technology skills, perhaps in test automation tools or software-defined infrastructure.

Strong technologists should always be able to learn the next test tool or programming language. When hiring into teams it is important to focus on the core attributes of the individual rather than hiring only for specific technologies.

These same specialised-generalist principles are also applied to managerial personnel. All managers are expected to have a strong knowledge of Agile and project and service management principles. In Enterprise Agile managers are expected to drive delivery, not just report on it. It is also likely that managers will have a specialism in the same way as 'T' shaped technologists do. For managers this may be expertise in infrastructure delivery or test management for example.

THE KEY DELIVERY ROLES

Certain key roles must be filled for teams to successfully build and run the product. Depending on the scale of the organisation and product, not all roles will map to different individuals. Some roles are also quite broad and in larger organisations will be split across several people.

As we have already discussed, the organisation has a role to play in setting certain boundaries and constraints for product teams as well as providing support and guidance.

Role	Responsibilities
Product Sponsor	• Provides funding • Governance oversight
Enterprise Architect	• Provides organisation constraints and alignment • Architectural governance oversight

Table 4-1 : Key Organisational-Level Roles

The Product Team requires effective leadership and roles in this space are pivotal. **Table 4-2** outlines the key roles involved in leading the product team. The emphasis here is on leadership rather than management. The leadership team charts a course for the product and empowers the delivery and support teams to do their daily work.

Role	Responsibilities
Product Owner	• Understands the business domain and user insights • Owns the Product Roadmap
Delivery Manager	• Plans and co-ordinates business and technical change • Manages change and service
Solution Architect	• Owns the big picture of the solution • Manages the technical governance process

Table 4-2 : Product Leadership Roles

The teams of technologists, domain specialist and customer support analysts deliver the real work of implementing and supporting change. The key roles within those teams are listed in **Table 4-3**.

Role	Responsibilities
Team Lead	• Guides the work of the team • Removes blockers and escalates issues
Technical Lead	• Coaches and mentors technologists • Owns the technical design
Analyst	• Organises user needs • Aligns delivery to outcomes
Developer	• Implements technical change • Maintains the delivery pipeline
Tester	• Develops approaches to build in quality • Creates and executes test packs
Support Analyst	• Receives and triages support incidents • Works with the team on problem management

Table 4-3 : Team Roles

FOCUSED DELIVERY TEAMS

The building block of the organisation for delivering technology change is the Delivery Team. These teams are deliberately constructed cohesive units working collaboratively towards common goals. There isn't a universally applicable formula for the type and number of individuals in the team, but there are some reasonable guidelines. Typically we expect to see Delivery Teams configured such that:

1. One individual can ably manage the team - this implies an optimal team size of about 8 ± 2.

2. It includes all the skills required to deliver an increment of technology change.

3. All are focused around a common goal – delivery of specified features.

Irrespective of method, all technology delivery comprises activities to analyse, develop, test, build and deploy. All of these activities need to be covered by the individuals within the team. By working together on the goal of delivering a feature to the user, these teams avoid the creation of the traditional silo mentality that has historically existed between functions such as Development and Test.

Figure 4-5 : Example Delivery Team Structure

Figure 4-5 provides an example of a technology Delivery Team with all the elements required to design, construct and deliver a solution to the user. Although there is no definitive formula, a good rule of thumb for the ratio of development, test and analysis is 4:2:1.

RESPONSIVE SERVICE TEAMS

Complementing the Delivery Teams in the Product Team are the Service Teams that operate the product and respond to user queries. These types of resources are also best grouped into manageable teams of around 8. Each team may contain a mix of resources who specialise in dealing with users and resolving incidents.

Where a defect is found the Service Team passes it to the Delivery Teams for resolution as it requires a change. In traditional IT support terms Service Teams undertake first and second line support, and Delivery Teams undertake third line support. Service Teams should include service agents who deal with customers and diagnose basic issues together with more technical resources who may use tools provided by the Delivery Teams, or the underlying platform to fix incidents.

As the Product Team scales, Service Teams may focus on particular groups of users or parts of the system. As with Delivery Teams, all the members of Service Teams are focused around a common goal – providing a great service for users.

EFFECTIVE TEAM LEADERSHIP

Getting the right people to lead teams is pivotal to success. There are two aspects to this which may or may not be filled by one person. Firstly a strong team lead is required to co-ordinate the activities of the team, track progress towards goals, and raise issues and remove blockers that impede delivery.

The second side to leadership is more technically biased, taking a lead on design, mentoring the team and upholding the constraints and standards set by the broader organisation. Often the best technologist in the team is not the right person to perform the former of these roles but would be suited to the latter.

ORGANISING CHANGE ACROSS DELIVERY TEAMS

When multiple Delivery Teams are engaged in delivering a product, a decision is required as to how to allocate work between them. There are two schools of thought:

1. The teams could have an affinity with components or parts of the system.

or

2. The teams could be organised around cohesive end-to-end features that cut across potential technology or component boundaries.

There isn't a definitive answer, although we have a preference for feature teams rather than component teams. There are advantages and disadvantages to each approach, as outlined in **Table 4-4**.

Feature Teams	Component Teams
Focused on end-to-end delivery and the common goal of creating business value.	Easier to allocate work across feature dependencies.
Clear responsibility over fixing issues, avoids defects being thrown 'over the wall'.	Allows specialist teams to work on specialist technologies.
Ensures continuous and regular integration across components.	Enables multi-speed delivery across different systems.
Creates greater awareness of full technology stack across the team.	May more efficiently facilitate sharing of components across multiple product teams.

Table 4-4 : Team Affinity

The key thing to remember is that success requires alignment of delivery model, team organisation, architecture and vendor management. If you engage multiple suppliers and they are providing expertise for specific elements of the technology stack then feature teams may not be the answer.

Real-world constraints often mean a hybrid model is used in many organisations. For example the software vendor may maintain the back office operational fulfilment package, while cohesive feature teams maintain multi-channel customer engagement systems. It is also possible for the position to move with time as early stages of delivering a new product requires focused work on frameworks.

Scaling the Model

When the overall product team becomes larger than around five delivery and service teams it is probably time to think about how to adapt the structure. Traditional thinking would suggest creating a hierarchy and an additional layer of management. To an extent there is no avoiding some form of organisational structure to coordinate across the growing team, but any structure should be lightweight and pass the Enterprise Agile 'Necessary and sufficient' test.

Several models have been offered by organisations employing large-scale agile delivery techniques. Some organisations employ terminology such as 'Clans' and 'Tribes' to describe groupings of teams. In Enterprise Agile we adopt the more straightforward nomenclature of Streams, Capabilities, Communities and Teams to describe bigger team structures and organisational containers.

A key driver in our thinking about larger teams is the balance between empowering people to take ownership of their work and quality of delivery, with the organisation's need for some consistency of approach and easily digestible information on status and progress. A key to success in larger teams is effective communication. Structured and formal channels should be supported by informal ad-hoc communications, enabled by the physical working environment and suitable tools.

In Enterprise Agile several key constructs help support the growing team:

Stream - a group of teams working on related functionality or components of the system.

Capability - a logical grouping of team members undertaking the same job function.

Community - a group of people with similar interests looking to promote improvements in a particular area.

Focused Streams of Activity

As the number of individual teams grow then these may require some logical grouping and additional co-ordination. For this purpose, we use the term 'Stream' to describe a collection of related teams. Teams may be grouped by function such as delivery, service and business change, by functional area or by technical component. There are clear advantages to each, however our preference is for functional area first and technical component second. We are keen to avoid silos and maintain the concept of tightly bound teams working toward common goals. To be successful, the organisation of Streams should align with technical architecture and any supplier model and incentives.

When there are several Streams each with a number of teams it may be necessary to replicate the product leadership function across each stream. This ensures that there is sufficient delivery management, solution architecture and product owner bandwidth to coordinate and lead the work of the team as illustrated in **Figure 4-6**.

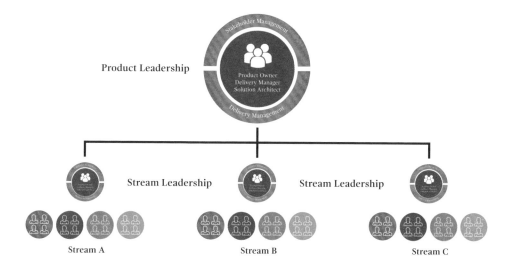

Figure 4-6 : Multiple Streams

LEADING CONSISTENCY THROUGH CAPABILITIES

When multiple teams exist it is useful to lead the work of the same job function across these teams. For example, a test capability may exist to group together the Testers across several teams and share best practice, ways of working and tools. A Test Lead may span the teams and provide guidance, co-ordinate and lead on working methods and provide a lightweight governance function.

This secondary alignment of the individual to a Capability, in addition to the primary role of delivering as part of the team, provides a useful matrix structure to support people in their daily work. The use of Capabilities is illustrated in **Figure 4-7**.

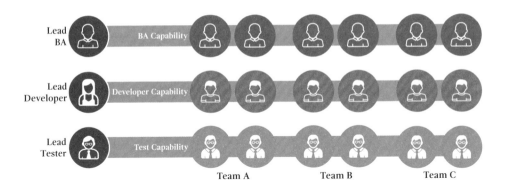

Figure 4-7 : Capability Leadership

Building Communities for Continuous Improvement

If, as we suggest, technologists are located within delivery teams tied to products then we hope that their primary affinity is to the product. Whilst this achieves focus on product delivery it is important for both the organisation and the individual that there is a broader fabric of community within the technology domain.

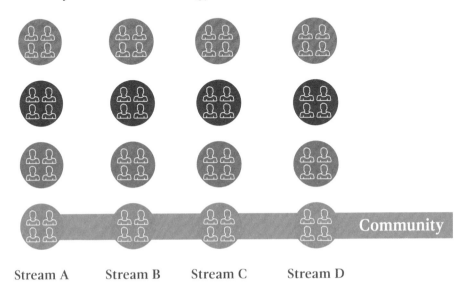

Figure 4-8 : Communities Across Multiple Teams and Products

Creating Communities for particular groups of individuals or specific skill areas helps develop people and the organisation through improved sharing of ideas and knowledge. It allows the organisation to experiment and innovate from the ground up supported by lightweight governance.

A typical way to build a Community is to encourage knowledge sharing through appropriate tools and to get together interested individuals from across different product teams on a regular basis. Ideas and improvements to working methods or tools identified by these groups are likely to pass through the appropriate governance process, such as a Technical Design Authority.

KEY POINTS

1 Team decisions and priorities should be guided and supported by the culture and values system of the organisation.

2 Delivery is ability-led and effective teams are made from 'T' shaped individuals who all have broad experience of Agile delivery coupled with a specialism.

3 Change and service should be delivered by cohesive teams with everyone working toward a common goal.

4 A strong leadership function, comprising Product Ownership, Delivery Management and Solution Architecture is required to drive delivery.

5 Build self-sustaining communities from the bottom up to share ideas and promote good practice within specific technical areas.

5

Effective Leadership

At the heart of a strong Product Team is a leadership function that can guide and direct delivery of features that meet user needs and add value to the organisation. The number and type of individual roles may vary according to the scale of the service provided and the structure of the delivery and operations functions.

Leaders need a full 360-degree view of any initiative in order to manage effectively both outwardly to stakeholders and also within the delivery team. They need to be capable of working with the broader organisation on strategy and to enable good governance. Effective leadership of empowered teams is where the most leverage is gained for organisations looking to thrive in the modern economy.

CONCEPTS

PROJECT AND SERVICE MANAGEMENT LEADERSHIP CONVERGENCE

Several recent innovations in technology are combining in a new model for building and running the products and services that organisations rely upon.

The rise of Cloud computing and the era of 'Software-defined everything' mean that software engineering practices are taking over the full technology stack and heavily influencing not just the build, but also the running of services - the DevOps model.

However, DevOps is not just about the technology of continuous delivery. It is a cultural and organisational shift that requires a new way of thinking about how to change and support products.

In addition to the expansion of software engineering practices into technical Operations, service management thinking is moving back up the line into delivery. The lifecycle of a product does not begin when software is delivered to Operations, but when an organisation conceives and initiates the production of the idea.

Traditionally the 'Build' of a product was separate from the operations required to 'Run' it. This led to two separate disciplines of Project Management and Service Management. Increasingly these areas overlap.

THREE KEY LEADERSHIP COMPONENTS

A good Product Team requires three elements of leadership, often provided by three or more individuals:

1. Delivery (project and service) management.

2. Product domain expertise.

3. Solution architecture.

Each has a role to play in working upward with the wider organisation and stakeholders and downward into the team delivering change and running the service.

Figure 5-1 : 360 Degree Product Leadership

The common responsibilities of each of the key leadership roles are explored in **Table 5-1**. Whilst the three leadership roles work together to change and support the product, the responsibilities we outline do imply some structure. Ultimately as the plan and budget holder, the Delivery Manager is accountable for the delivery of changes and the service for the product. This does not necessarily mean there is a strict reporting line from the Solution Architect and the Product Owner into the Delivery Manager. Sometimes this relationship can be a complex dynamic, for example the Product Owner being provided by the organisation and

Delivery Manager and Solution Architect being from a third party supplier.

Delivery Manager	Product Owner	Solution Architect
Outward Responsibilities		
Manage allocated resource and budget.	Understand and prioritise user needs.	Actively manage technical risk.
Reporting including service KPIs and delivery metrics.	Contribute to organisational strategy. Communicate with the customer.	Product alignment with enterprise architecture.
Escalate risk and issues to the organisation.		Contribute to the technology community.
Inward Responsibilities		
Remove delivery blockers from the team.	Ensure common understanding of user needs.	Coach and support teams in understanding the overall solution architecture.
Manage and motivate the team.	Make priority calls on delivery.	
Own the plan.	Support test and assurance activities.	Promote good practice and awareness of enterprise architecture.
		Review and contribute to detailed design work.

Table 5-1 : Responsibilities of Key Roles

The most important point is that all three areas must work together to deliver a product focused on user needs that adds value to the organisation.

NECESSARY AND SUFFICIENT GOVERNANCE

Governance often has a bad reputation amongst Delivery Teams. It conjures up thoughts of bureaucracy, red tape and reasons not to do things. We have already established that the modern organisation needs to change at a faster pace and continually evolve its products to meet user needs. In order to do so, the role of governance must be to guide and support with judicious management of risk.

Infrequent, onerous approval gates are replaced by lightweight regular guidance. This requires a mind-set change for sponsors and executives. Teams must be trusted to deliver and provided with regular support to do their job. Executives have a responsibility to the organisation to manage risk and ensure resources are used effectively. Discharging this responsibility requires engagement and strong leadership.

Teams have a part to play in building this trusted relationship through demonstrating value-add to the organisation and by being open and transparent about challenges that exist. The judgement required here is a key skill of the leadership team. Too often change initiatives spiral out of control due to a loss of confidence by stakeholders. This often becomes a bigger problem than any underlying delivery issue. Teams need to demonstrate they are in control whilst not hiding problems.

ESTIMATING WORK

One of our aims for this book is to help organisations build predictability into their delivery process. The techniques we describe can help with this and a key point is to break change down into smaller pieces, and release often. Another essential factor is the process by which work is estimated and sized, particularly when this is being undertaken to advise funding for a MVP.

Traditional project planning relies on decomposing the perceived work and then estimating based on the effort (in man days) required to complete. The drawback with such work breakdown structures is that they require significant upfront discovery work and assume that functionality is relatively fixed. Both of these factors do not really lend themselves to Agility.

Alternative Agile methods of estimation take a more holistic approach, sizing pieces of work based on relative complexity to get an overall view of the effort required. A common method is to use Story Points to mark the relative complexity of functional units (Stories). Typically the numbers used are something like a Fibonacci sequence (1, 2, 3, 5, 8, 13, 21, 34) to demonstrate increasing uncertainty in larger Stories.

The strength of Story Points as an abstract concept can also become a significant weakness during Delivery. We have seen many projects go awry due to the intangible nature of the metrics being used. For small scale change and the work of a small team, simple use of Story Points and a velocity (the rate at which Story Points are currently being delivered) may work. The drawbacks of Story Points on larger programmes and MVP delivery can be significant and do not aid predictability, notably:

1. Many business sponsors do not understand the abstract concept of Story Points and want (need) to work in clear effort and monetary terms.

2. Story Points can lead to a lack of transparency over progress, particularly when they are diluted through re-estimation. Delivery of Story Points gives the illusion of progress even though the backlog is not reducing.

We would urge extreme caution when using Story Points particularly in conjunction with third party suppliers and contracts. Delivery of Story Points does not always equate to progress towards the end goal and is certainly not a measure of supplier productivity.

The Enterprise Agile Approach

Taking a Risk-First Approach

We are strong advocates of active risk management and a risk-first approach to delivery. Risk takes many forms. Some risks are under the control of the Product Team, some they can influence and others are external to the organisation that they are unable to affect.

When considering implementing change to a product it is essential to take time to consider risk, its source, and what can be done to influence or manage it. Taking a risk-first approach means tackling unknowns early, providing the opportunity to fail fast or adjust plans while there is still time to do so.

In practical terms the risk-first approach means that everyone in the team is actively engaged in applying their skill and judgment to recognise potential risks and consider innovative approaches to address them. It is this area where the Delivery Manager is expected to make a significant contribution. We believe that managers should be actively driving towards no surprises in delivering change, not simply reporting on it. The Manager is expected to fly ahead of the team to look for potential obstacles.

The Enterprise Agile approach includes the following elements to help realise the risk-first principle:

1. **The Product Lifecycle**
   Use of Feasibility and Discovery phases ahead of Delivery to manage risk to MVP delivery.

2. **The Delivery Pipeline**
   Fully automated software build and deployment using repeatable processes rather than manual error-prone alternatives.

3. **Quality Built-In**
   Well thought through test approaches to ensure a high quality product is delivered and assured.

4. **Architecture Centric**
   Proving architecture early in the product lifecycle and ensuring that architecture evolves in a controlled manner.

5. **Sprint Planning**
   Making sure the high risk areas of technical or functional delivery are addressed in the early Sprints of the release.

IMPLEMENTING GOOD GOVERNANCE

Delivery teams are often required to conform to the constraints of an existing governance framework. In the Agile organisation, governance is still required and serves an essential function. Good governance is about timely support and interventions rather than cumbersome processes and gates designed to minimise risk, whilst introducing considerable overhead.

Governance will consist of lightweight regular forums between the product leadership and executive sponsors and stakeholders. The governance process should fulfil three key aims:

1. **Inform** – Provide suitable performance indicators.

2. **Escalate** – A route up in the organisation to raise critical issues.

3. **Assure** – Keep the product aligned to organisation goals.

Inevitably governance will involve some form of regular meetings to discuss status and key risks and issues. We believe that these should be focused and lightweight with issues raised by exception. It is also desirable that such sessions are reasonably frequent - where Sprint delivery is used, aligning to Sprint delivery and governance can be useful.

BRIDGING TO THE ORGANISATION

The key governance review meeting between the Product Team and organisation executives is the Programme/Project Board or perhaps more appropriate in an Agile organisation, the Product Governance Board. This provides the Product Team the opportunity to request additional support from the sponsor and to raise issues. The board performs the function of steering product development and levels of service received by the end users. Conflicting priorities may be escalated to this group for guidance.

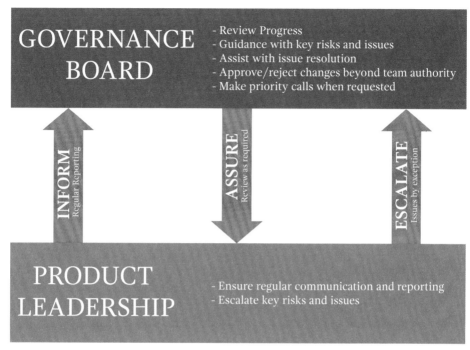

Figure 5-2 : Flow Between Governance Board and Product Team

Diligence Within the Product Team

Good governance is also important within the Product Team itself, particularly as it grows. One area we believe that some ceremony is required is design decision-making. Using a Design Authority to record key design decisions is a powerful tool to help plot and record the course the product takes over time.

There are two facets to the Design Authority: functional design decisions and technical design decisions. We recommend both are discussed at the same forum. Taking decisions in isolation of a discussion about delivery impact should be avoided. This group should be diverse and include those managing the delivery of change, not just the technical and analyst Community.

The frequency of the product design authority meetings may vary. The more intense the phase of delivery and volume of change, the more frequent the meetings are likely to be. This keeps change flowing and minimises the amount of decisions at any one time.

The workings of the Design Authority are likely to be tied to the Sprint delivery pattern. This ensures that areas of design related to work for the following Sprint can be guided as necessary as requirements are further elaborated. The Design Authority will operate within organisational constraints such as Enterprise Architecture.

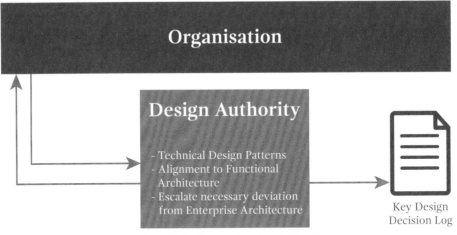

Figure 5-3 : Product Design Authority

THE ON-GOING IMPORTANCE OF PLANNING

Agility does not mean foregoing a plan. Managing change requires planning, but the real measure of success is demonstrable progress towards the required outcomes. No team should slavishly follow a plan without reference to defined goals. The level of planning depends on the scale of the change and the level of Agility across the organisation.

Roadmaps typically exist at organisation and product level. A roadmap is a statement of intent and suggests a phasing and rough timing for initiatives. A plan is more concrete. It implies commitment and identifies who does what, by when.

Products that are relatively standalone and mature can evolve through continuous product innovation and require little planning. The replacement of a legacy system with a big bang cutover and a number of third party dependencies requires much more work. Planning is usually most important during the inception of a product and getting to MVP and launch.

We recommend that plans are layered with successive levels of refinement. For the majority of small initiatives a single level Sprint plan is often sufficient. For large scale changes there are commonly three layers of planning that roll up into each other.

High level Plan

Planning at a high level will capture the major milestones and interactions with other products and services across the organisation and any external dependencies. This high level plan is generally outside the remit of the Product Team and manages portfolio-level dependencies. This plan is key for larger scale change programmes and is often expressed as a flight plan to bring together multiple, related work streams and products.

Mid level Plan

The mid tier of planning focuses on the work of the entire Product Team, their interactions with each other and the bringing together of business and technical change. This artefact is the key guide for the Product Team and is owned by the Delivery Manager with input from all the team leaders. It is this plan that the governance process tracks against.

Low level Plan

A low level plan looks at the day-to-day work of individual teams delivering change and supporting the product. This layer is the most fluid and often exists within the delivery pipeline tooling. This equates to the individual Sprint Plan used to deliver change and release increments of the Product.

Planning Across Lifecycle Phases

The role and level of planning evolves across the lifecycle.

Feasibility

At the Feasibility stage the key activities are understanding the objectives of the initiative. Feasibility can often be brief, perhaps even only a few days and a handful of people. Planning activities at this stage involve ensuring that key stakeholders are engaged, the candidate delivery options are validated and understood and a suitable proposal for delivery is prepared.

Much of the effort in Feasibility should focus on building a robust plan for Discovery that allows for that phase to conclude successfully.

Discovery

A number of essential objectives must be achieved during Discovery - an intensive phase designed to reduce risk and increase predictability during Delivery.

Where Discovery is more than a couple of weeks duration, a Discovery phase plan should begin the operation of a Sprint pattern. This allows for Agile principles of a regular heartbeat to facilitate course corrections and demonstrable progress.

In essence Discovery is concerned at a high level with **what** the initiative is about, **how** will it be done (both solution architecture and delivery approach), and what **measures** will be put in place to ensure successful delivery.

Delivery

The Delivery plan is a Sprint-based plan that, whilst allowing for refinement and change, is aimed at providing some degree of predictability – particularly up to the point of MVP. An initial Sprint plan for MVP is built during Discovery. Following MVP launch, a Sprint plan may only extend as far as the next release or few Sprints.

Generating a Sprint Plan

It is useful to have a view a few Sprints ahead in order to be able to link Agile product delivery with other fixed, real-world dependencies. One scenario where a Sprint plan is most useful for a longer duration is in the delivery of an MVP. This is generally because the initial product delivery has some fairly challenging real-world constraints and deadlines and the organisation is seeking a greater degree of predictability.

Creating a Sprint plan for MVP is relatively straightforward provided suitable structured analysis has been undertaken and there is a set of estimates against the required scope. Developing the plan is then simply a matter of allocating work to Sprints based on resource capacity for the duration.

Estimating for MVP

The bulk of the effort to create an initial Sprint plan for MVP is identifying the features required and estimating the work involved. The process of generating the scope for MVP and structuring requirements is covered in more detail in Chapter 6.

Assuming that the Analysis work has produced a backlog of Epic features to deliver, a good way to generate the estimates for the plan is to take a top-down approach and 'shirt size' the requirements. The Discovery phase of the product lifecycle should yield a functional scope against which to estimate. There are three distinct stages of creating the estimate.

Build the Model

The build of the model is a case of listing out all of the feature Epics and applying a shirt size to them. We normally use five shirt sizes; XS, S, M, L, XL. It is often useful at this stage to adopt a blind estimating technique where members of the team do not compare results until the exercise is completed, so as not to bias each other.

After this stage we have identified the relative complexity of the Epics and flushed out any unknowns. It is also possible to see the potential variance based on different estimator's understanding of the problem.

Calibrate the Model

In order to make the model useful we need to assign numbers to it. To do this we will take a representative sample, perhaps up to 20% of the Epics, and decompose them into Stories. These Stories are then sized in ideal days. It is essential as this stage to take a representative set of Epics across the product and of different shirt sizes.

From this stage of the process we can determine the average effort required for the delivery of each size and get an overall effort for the MVP in ideal days. Factoring in an efficient ratio and capacity for defects allows a total required capacity to be attained and a Sprint plan built.

Test the Model

There is no substitute for doing actual work to determine the accuracy of the estimation model. For a large product build it is likely that certain elements of the solution will be prototyped during Discovery. These pieces of work could be used to recalibrate the model.

Generally, the resources applied to Discovery are likely to be more experienced and the items tackled more complex, so using unadjusted Discovery phase actuals to recalibrate the entire model may be unwise. Certainly delivery metrics from the first few Sprints should be fed back. It is also worth bearing in mind that the productivity of new teams, whilst initially low, will increase during the early stages of delivery.

MANAGING CHANGES TO THE PLAN

The purpose of greater Agility in the organisation is to allow for flexibility and responsiveness to adapt to evolving user needs. In this environment change is inevitable and should be encouraged.

There does however need to be some direction and stability as provided by the roadmaps and plans created for individual products. Whilst Product Teams should be empowered to do the things that users need and release value for the organisation, change should not be unconstrained.

Where a baseline scope has been created for a Product Increment or MVP then it may be necessary to use Change Control to govern this. The use of a Change Control process ensures that any revised scope remains true to the organisation's goals and that any outside dependencies can be adjusted. It also allows for expectations to be managed if particular large features come in or out of scope, adjusting delivery dates or the need for (interim) manual processes.

Minor changes as a result of regular story elaboration and items moving between Sprints would not normally require Change Control. It is the major scope changes at Epic level that require visibility and more formal decision-making.

ACTIVE RAID MANAGEMENT FOR IMPROVED PREDICTABILITY

Even if you are able to embrace continuous product innovation and exploit Agile techniques across the organisation, you will still face changes presented by the outside world. Active RAID (Risks, Assumptions, Issues and Dependencies) management is still as important as ever to avoid unpleasant surprises.

We often find that these terms are misused, so it's worth a quick recap of the definitions.

Term	Definition	Example
Risk	An identified threat to delivery.	The supplier may not be able to provide suitably skilled resources at the right time.
Assumption	A documented expectation based on the facts available at the time. A change to the assumption could jeopardise delivery.	There will be no regulatory or compliance changes during the delivery project.
Issue	An actual problem that impedes delivery.	An issue has been identified in a core foundation technology product that inhibits the non-functional requirements being met.
Dependency	Required input from elsewhere within or outside of the organisation. Dependencies should have a due date.	The procurement agreement with the Cloud service provider will be signed by 1st Jan 2018.

Table 5-2 : RAID Definitions

Materialised risks, false assumptions and missed dependencies all result in issues. Teams also identify blockers through their daily stand-up meetings. Blockers that cannot be dealt with through team interaction also need to be raised and recorded as issues.

REPORTING

A key part of the leadership role on a Product Team is timely and accurate reporting to enable fact-based decision making and any required interventions. When too little or too much information is provided, time-poor stakeholders get frustrated at not being able to rapidly understand the current position. It is essential that the leadership team articulates a clear story about the state of the service and change initiatives. This narrative is supported by a number of relevant KPIs and metrics.

Definition	Example
Summary	Narrative to briefly describe current status.
RAG status	Red/Amber/Green to reflect current product status often split into sub-categories: • Progress • Quality • Service • Value • Team • Suppliers
Work planned / done	Outline of the work planned for the reporting period and the work actually complete.
Key RAID changes	Any significant movement in RAID.

Metrics	Key metrics and trends that support the current position on delivery of change and service include:
	
	• **Progress**
	  - Sprint Burn-down
	  - Release Burn-up
	
	• **Quality**
	  - Defect find/fix rate
	  - System availability
	
	• **Service**
	  - Volume of incidents
	  - Performance against SLAs

Table 5-3 : Suggested Reporting Contents

Concern arises when information is reported that does not represent the complete picture. This can quickly become a distraction and result in demands for further information. Before long the Product Team is spending a disproportionate amount of time servicing questions rather than delivering. In the absence of the right information, stakeholders make judgements based on perceptions. If this point is reached it is time to stop, take stock and agree a recovery plan to remedy the key issues and return to fact-based conversations.

Metrics and data collection for reporting should be built into the delivery tooling and, as far as possible, be automated. Minimal effort is required from the team to record the tasks being worked on if the tools are set up correctly from the outset. It should be clear that delivery metrics are best used to understand rate of progress and product quality to aid planning, rather than a stick with which to beat team members. Reporting should echo the message coming out of the Sprint ceremonies such as estimation and planning meetings and Show and Tells.

A good report will include the key elements described in **Table 5-3**.

Keep the Information Flowing

Whilst regular reporting is required to keep stakeholders informed, this should not be the sole source of information. Delivery, service and quality metrics should be always visible to the team and stakeholders.

There should be no surprises for anyone in terms of status of delivery and progress towards agreed goals. The use of whiteboards and preferably screens in the team environment is to be encouraged. It is straightforward to get most modern tooling to display a dashboard to highlight progress, quality and service metrics.

The current delivery position should always be very visible to teams. Everyone is signed up to working towards a set of common goals and progress towards these should be of interest to everyone.

KEY POINTS

1 A strong leadership function should cover three components; Delivery Management, Product Ownership and Solution Architecture.

2 'Necessary and sufficient' governance should be put in place with clearly defined paths for Information, Escalation and Assurance.

3 Estimation for MVP involves building, calibrating and testing a model based on the Discovery phase feature backlog.

4 An initial Sprint plan for delivering an MVP is required and this is built during the Discovery Phase.

5 Active Risk, Issue, Assumption and Dependency management is still required in Agile delivery, particularly in the bridge to the non-Agile world.

6

Analysing User Needs

The clear reason to innovate, embrace technology and frequently change products is to add value to the organisation. This can only be achieved by getting closer to what users need and understanding how this can generate a valuable outcome. This requires insight into your market and user needs. The closer the organisation is to meeting the needs of its customers, the more likely it is to attract and retain them and fend off competition from disruptive business models.

Maintaining user focus requires a range of skills and tools. Traditionally the role of determining what the market and customers want has fallen to the Marketing function, while the role of defining changes to business processes and systems to Business Analysts. These roles continue to exist but must evolve to provide the Agility required for the organisation to rapidly change.

Concepts

Defining Stories With the Users

A key focus for all Agile methodologies is working in close collaboration with users to create a product that meets their needs. The most common output from this process is the User Story. A Story is a brief description of a function that the user wishes to perform that can be passed to the delivery team to build. An important aspect of a Story is that it is written in plain language that can be easily understood by everyone, rather than in any specific notation or diagrams that can only be interpreted by technologists. The principle of working closely with end users is a central tenet of Agile. It enables a lean way of working by cutting out the middle man, accelerating the traditional requirements capture process and increasing its accuracy.

Throughout this chapter we address this process in more detail and explain why simply writing Stories based on user input alone is often insufficient. In particular we focus on addressing three key points:

1. User Needs must be validated as 'Needs' rather than 'Wants', and linked to organisational goals. The purpose of delivering change is to add value to the organisation, not just to do what the user wants.

2. Stories on their own are not adequate unless a product is mature and the change is very small. Most user journeys and meaningful features will be described in several related Stories.

3. In many organisations the delivery team will not have free rein to talk to the users who are often too busy with their day jobs to participate.

BJSS Opinion

Who is the User?

It is important to note that the user can be anyone who interacts with the products or services provided by the organisation. These users can be internal or external to the organisation.

External users come in many forms. The most obvious being customers (B2B), consumers (B2C) and citizens (G2C). Other key external users might also include regulatory bodies and community groups.

Internal users are also a diverse group and include Operations, Finance, Logistics and Management groups. Surprisingly a group of internal users often overlooked by technology delivery is technology operations. Involving those who support the product in the delivery of change is essential for success – a key reason we advocate moving to a DevOps culture and associated practices.

Being Outcome-Led

In specifying change it is all too easy to let the work of defining requirements drift into defining the solution. In our analysis work we prefer to concentrate on the outcomes we aim to achieve for the users and the organisation. Focusing on outcomes elevates the language and conversation towards the 'Why' and 'What' rather than 'How'.

The overarching goals and outcomes for the organisation provide an important reference. Clearly defined outcomes assist with validating the more granular analysis activities and assurance work.

Who Determines User Needs?

There are several sources of information on what the user needs, and the role and relative importance these play varies depending upon the product and the type of user.

Where existing services are being enhanced, the business processes and usage patterns of the current system are likely to be key to understanding the behaviour and requirements of users. Dropouts and long dwell times in particular parts of an interface, for example, may highlight problems in the user experience that can be reviewed and inform enhancement requirements.

We would expect to see that the needs of external users are researched and informed by focus groups, data and insight gained from market research. Fresh input and feedback from users is now almost instant. Changes to a mobile app prompt immediate ratings and reviews. The advent of Big Data and analytics has meant that more than ever it is possible to obtain rich information about the behaviours and needs of a target market. Information gathered from social media and competing products is also likely to provide insight into user needs. We expect the Marketing and Digital functions of the organisation to be heavily involved in shaping this, and see them as an integral part of the product team.

Working with internal users in a large organisation can be a challenge - they are often busy running their day-to-day operations. Where possible a subject matter expert (SME) who knows the product well will work within the team responsible for the change. This is not always possible and it often falls to the Business Analysts to act as proxies and, through shadowing, interviewing and running workshops, determine the needs of internal users and act on their behalf.

With many sources of information and requirements, some structure is required to ensure a balanced view. This is a key role for the Analyst in the team. Remember the organisation is not commissioning change just to meet user needs - its primary reason is to generate business value.

It is important through assurance and governance that the valuable input provided by an SME is aligned with overall business outcomes. It can be easy for the users' wish list to dominate and cause a drift in vision. Effort is required to avoid the desire for perfection, and release change early and often in order to start generating value.

THE ROLE OF PRODUCT OWNER

The Product Owner is a key role in overseeing any change. This person is the day-to-day decision maker on priorities and what the user does, and does not, get from the product at a point in time. The Product Owner will work in collaboration with the Solution Architect and Delivery Manager to manage change.

We find that challenges often arise if the Product Owner is not suitably empowered, or conversely is too independent. Decisions regarding functional scope made in isolation of the broader governance oversight can give rise to problems. The Product Owner and the sponsor or budget holder are unlikely to be the same individual. The Product Owner must act within the governance framework and the tolerances of the organisation. This dynamic requires careful monitoring such that user needs are met and business outcomes are achieved whilst ensuring that Agility is not lost and budget control is retained.

Securing Engagement and Support

Business Analysts are often used as the bridge between 'the business' and technology teams when it comes to delivery. As we have already discussed we prefer to organise teams around products and use this convergence of different functions to break down barriers. In doing so, everyone is focused on the common goal of delivering change that adds value to the organisation by meeting user needs.

It is not always possible or desirable to be organised in this way - internal users and SMEs are often busy with their day job and may only be partly, if at all, allocated to change activities. Other factors often come into play in large organisations such as contractual obligations across suppliers where these users belong to a third party organisation.

Irrespective of the organisation structure, success in any change initiative, large or small, requires collaboration between all parties. We have always found that this requires investment in relationships and takes some time to achieve. The most effective and simple way of doing this is through regular engagement, transparency, and results.

We recommend that stakeholders, users and SMEs are actively involved and invited to regular demonstrations as part of the iterative delivery process. Through this engagement and seeing their input and feedback being taken on board, coupled with demonstration of real progress, this key stakeholder group will engage and actively participate.

A Structured Approach to Analysis

We are often asked to review programmes and recover projects. On almost all of these occasions a key factor contributing to delivery issues is poor specification of user needs. A lack of clarity of the outcomes required can only lead to problems further down the line. The old adage 'garbage in, garbage out' applies. If the analysis is unsound then delivery teams have little chance of achieving the outcomes the organisation is seeking.

For small-scale changes to relatively small products then simple User Story definition will be a suitable technique to capture and describe user needs. For most change, a more structured approach to analysis is required. Structured analysis is important because it:

1. Delivers a framework by which technical (system) and business (manual) change can be aligned and implemented effectively.

2. Enables the organisation to make priority calls based on which features can deliver the most value.

3. Allows inter-dependencies between features to be identified and informs allocation of work to delivery teams.

4. Provides a basis for estimating the size of the changes and the capacity required in the delivery teams.

5. Allows a link back to technical and functional architecture to inform the view of the risk associated with the change.

6. Provides traceability and a mechanism to track the progress of the change through delivery within the context of the problem domain.

7. Adds rigour to the analysis process and makes it more effective.

8. Provides assurance that the right questions have been asked and the appropriate sources consulted.

9. Documents in a lightweight manner the decisions that have been taken and the route to arriving at a particular functional solution.

Achieving all of these outcomes is essential for success.

BALANCING UPFRONT AND DEFERRED DISCOVERY

When considering any reasonable amount of change a balance must be struck between how much discovery occurs upfront against how much is deferred. Some Agile methodologies advocate beginning implementation immediately and undertaking all discovery during delivery. We favour a more balanced approach with some work upfront.

Choosing the right balance requires skill and judgement and depends on the type of change being undertaken, how it is funded and how value is to be realised. A large change programme to replace a legacy technology system will require upfront discovery and other activities to de-risk delivery. Small changes to an existing product that are released as they are developed require little upfront discovery.

Our approach is to ensure that the breadth of the requirement is understood at a high level before starting significant delivery work. This helps to establish scope and build a framework for structured analysis to track against during delivery. In addition high risk and a representative sample of functional areas are explored in more detail. This 'depth' pass across selected user needs de-risks delivery and aids the building of an estimation model with confidence.

Figure 6-1 : Discovery on a Large Change Programme

For large scale change programmes we adopt the pattern illustrated in **Figure 6-1**. By the end of the Discovery phase we would expect the breadth of the requirements at a high level to be enumerated such that the scope of the change is known. Elaboration of user needs in more detail will occur during iterative delivery, concluding prior to the end of Delivery. Non-functional requirements will be captured and defined in parallel with a good understanding of these developed by the end of Discovery.

The Enterprise Agile Approach

Introducing the Building Blocks of Good Analysis

Our approach to defining user needs aligned to organisation outcomes is based on the structured and layered analysis techniques described in this section. Within this model are a number layers we expect to see.

1. **Goals**
   The most important layer includes the organisational and user goals that any change initiative is seeking to achieve. These goals articulate the benefit and value of making any change.

2. **User Journey**
   A User Journey defines a business process or user interaction with the system. These may be long running transactions, such as placing an online order, from browsing to fulfilment. For internal systems these are the individual business processes that describe the function of that part of the organisation.

3. **Feature**
   A Feature is a coarse-grained function that realises a particular step in the User Journey. It is often at this level that the user wishes to see change and can recognise the value delivered. Whilst it can be possible to deliver value for a Story, on larger scale change initiatives completed Features are often required before a Product Increment is shipped.

4. **Epic**
   An Epic is an intermediate step between Feature and Stories. It may not always exist and is only usually required on large deliveries. Epics are typically mega-Stories that require further decomposition, but are useful as part of the analysis and estimation process.

5. **Story**
   The User Story is the familiar Agile requirement definition. It is this level of detail that is processed by individual teams to deliver change. There is a widely recognised syntax and structure for a User Story, described in **Figure 6-3**.

6. **Task**

A Task is a unit of work undertaken by engineers. Tasks are identified by teams during the Sprint planning process that we describe in more detail in Chapter 7. A Sprint is a time-boxed period used to deliver change and set a delivery cadence.

LAYERED REQUIREMENTS FOR MODELLING CHANGE

Our approach to specifying change is based on a structured and layered model for analysis. This method is shown in further detail in **Figure 6-2**. The model described is a scalable approach, at one end of the spectrum it will cater for a significant MVP on a large transformation project and at the other, a single simple enhancement.

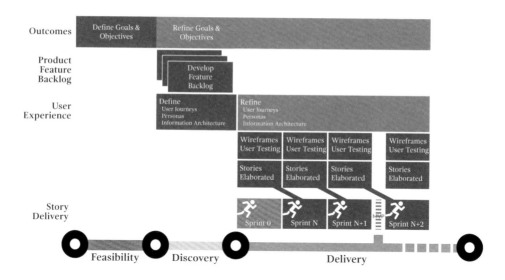

Figure 6-2 : Layered Requirements Analysis

Key to this model is that all changes expressed as User Stories link back through the layers to an organisation-level goal. This is an essential part of our process. It is not good enough during requirements elaboration to just write down Stories based on what a user might want. User needs must be linked to an outcome.

This model works equally well for various application types and internal and external users. In each case the user has an outcome in mind and a process or set of steps to follow to reach this outcome. Each major step in the process is a Feature that has some value. It is these Features that are then further decomposed into Epics and Stories that can be estimated and delivered by the team in Sprints.

The User Story

The basic building block for defining a requirement is a User Story. Stories are often written on cards to put up on a whiteboard or captured in an Agile planning tool. User Stories are equally useful for capturing work that is to be done by a manual process as well as that which will be coded up and delivered by technology. Stories are written using the '*As A [Who], I Want [What], so That [Why]*' syntax. User Stories should also include Acceptance Criteria so that is it is possible to check the requirement has been met.

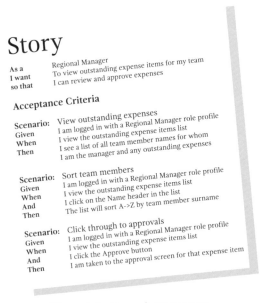

Figure 6-3 : Example User Story

Tracking Progress Towards Meeting User Needs

Another common problem we find when reviewing projects is that it is often difficult to articulate exactly what progress has been made towards the required outcomes. Using structured analysis techniques allows a baseline of the breadth (scope) of the proposed change to be created. Requirements are further refined as delivery teams proceed with the implementation.

We find that even on projects with good delivery metrics it is often difficult to describe to stakeholders exactly what has been done. Numbers alone do not paint a sufficiently rich picture and must be augmented by context. The regular demonstrations of the solution through iterative Show and Tell meetings help provide this context, but on large change initiatives progress must be tracked against the bigger picture.

Consider implementing a new digital channel for a hotel provider. This may have three key functional areas - customer account management, search and book, and customer service. These areas may each have a different number of Customer Journeys, each of which is described by a different number of Epics. Being able to represent this visually as in **Figure 6-4** creates a map towards meeting user needs and is much more powerful for conveying the status to stakeholders than metrics. Statistics such as 6 of 10 Epics completed or a velocity of 26 Story points are often not understood by stakeholders, who are interested in progress within the context of the business domain. Spatial awareness is also very powerful for visualising the work done against the estimated size of each area.

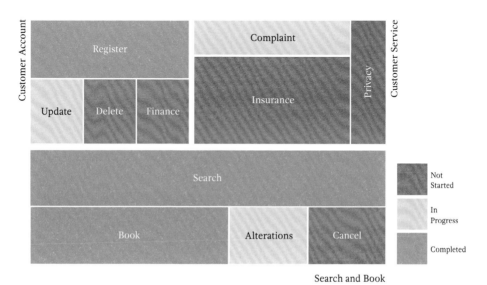

Figure 6-4 : Visual Progress Mapping Against Structured Analysis

Accounting for all User Needs

We often observe the functional requirements of end users being considered separately from the non-functional requirements of technical users. There is some sense in this but all user needs should be assessed and prioritised according to the value delivered.

If, for example, there is a technical Story to replace a software component due to security concerns or licensing costs, then the value of doing this must be assessed alongside traditional functional stories to meet end user needs.

Some analysis work may lead to identification of requirements that are simply constraints, such as particular technology choices from the organisation's enterprise architecture function or reporting requirements from a regulator. These are user needs too, but there is no real option not to meet or to de-prioritise them if your organisation operates in a regulated industry.

It is important to be aware of the desired non-functional behaviour of any technology solution upfront - it is much harder to adapt to refinements and discovery of these during the implementation of a change. The difference between a 1 second or a 1 milli-second response time is likely to impact the choice of underlying technologies, potentially causing significant rework and delay.

Aligning Business and Technical Change

Inevitably some user needs will be met by delivering technology and others by implementing or modifying business processes. The Product Owner, working within the defined governance framework, will determine which user needs will be met by technology and those that will not. We recommend that manual processes, training and people change activities are implemented iteratively in parallel with the technology changes.

Maintaining a joined-up approach to business and technology change is essential to avoid divergent outcomes or gaps appearing. Refinement of detail as implementation of the change progresses allows for the boundary between technology delivery and business change activities to be adjusted. This can only be achieved through the application of a structured analysis approach. We expect to see business change teams working alongside technology teams throughout delivery.

A WORD OR TWO ABOUT ARTEFACTS

The Agile manifesto states a preference for working software over comprehensive documentation. We are also generally in favour of getting the job done rather than creating documentation, however embracing Agility should not mean 'no documentation'. Creating artefacts that can be used to distribute information and record it for the future to support delivery teams is always required. The art is in determining the 'Necessary and sufficient' breadth and depth of documentation.

Maintaining documents is rarely done effectively and is not a good approach. As change initiatives move through the various phases it is often best to document for that point in time. Typically we would consider documenting at three key points in delivery.

1. Document what the user needs.

2. Produce the artefacts that support teams during the delivery of the change.

3. Document what work was done in order to support the change.

We would expect these activities to occur repeatedly across cycles of change. Creating fixed documents that are published and go stale should be avoided in favour of living artefacts supported by the appropriate tools.

DESIGNING A COMPELLING USER EXPERIENCE

The Product Owner will determine how user needs are best met in order to maximise value for the organisation. Clearly there is considerable scope for interpreting how to meet the needs of the user and indeed how to account for the differing needs across the entire user base. It is therefore essential that a mechanism exists to capture not only the needs of the user but to check during delivery that perception and implementation are aligned. In addition, the actual interface through which external users interact with the organisation, be that through technology or people, should be optimised to suit the style of the users.

For large pieces of work, User Experience Design may be a specialist role within the delivery team. More likely it is federated across the wider group. In either case there are a number of key areas to address:

1. Know the User

Through interviews and regular engagement, get to know the user. Develop personas as an aid to teams to keep the real users in mind.

2. Analyse Data

Use data from usage patterns and other relevant sources to gain insight into what your user really does and needs. Use this to generate business outcomes and value.

3. Make use of Mock-ups

Before investing too heavily in building anything, construct lightweight models, prototypes and mock-ups to solicit user feedback and inform teams what to build.

4. Usability Testing

Create and test alternative journeys and visual layouts with real users to arrive at the optimal experience.

5. Keep the User Involved

Keep users engaged throughout delivery. Obtain feedback and use it to refine the implementation of the change during delivery.

Creating Understanding With Cohorts

User communities (internal and external) can be large. It is not always possible to engage with every user to determine their needs and understand what would create a compelling user experience for them. It is important to consult with each type of user. We refer to each related user group as a Cohort.

For internal users these might be people in the same department or job function, for example, sales order entry or credit control. Cohorts group similar users who undertake tasks in a defined part of the overall business process. In an online ordering system for example, there are groups of users who curate the online product catalogue, undertake fulfilment and logistics and manage accounts and payment processing. All users are focused on a common goal of fulfilling the order, but grouping them together in this way allows for better integration of system and manual processes, facilitating more effective business change and a better user experience.

For external users the landscape is often more rich and diverse and Cohorts are sometimes formed to group similar types of customers. Cohorts may exist for geo-demographic profiling, customer loyalty or many other categories as fits the purpose of the organisation. It is likely that customers could belong to multiple Cohorts across different categories and also move between these over time. This grouping can enable personalisation of the products offered and allow the organisation to get closer to the individual need, improving the experience and value generated. A thorough exploration of market segmentation and data marketing is beyond the scope of this book. What is important as you move closer to technology delivery is that a clear understanding of the Cohorts exists, such that their impact on system behaviour can be defined.

The Power of the Persona

We find it powerful to build a life-like picture of an example user from each Cohort. These personas help delivery teams to have a real view of the people they are implementing change for and to work with real names rather than generic users.

Developing personas for users and displaying them on the wall where the delivery teams work is a useful approach.

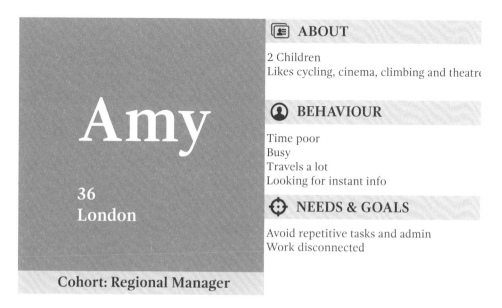

Figure 6-5 : Example Persona

KEY POINTS

1 Analysis isn't simply a matter of documenting user needs as stories - all functional and non-functional requirements need to deliver value.

2 Use a structured and layered analysis approach to break down business outcomes into Features, Epics, Stories and delivery Tasks.

3 Cohorts and Personas provide a very powerful technique for grouping users and bringing them to life for the delivery team.

4 Structured analysis forms the basis of 'in context' status reporting to provide a meaningful visual indicator of progress.

5 Ensure that all user needs are catered for during analysis activities, including operational and non-functional requirements.

7

Crafting the Product Increment

New increments of functionality are periodically released to users by the Product Team. This increment may consist of technological enhancements or new features. Irrespective of delivery method, the new features help evolve the product in ways that improve the experience for the user, address an unmet need and add value to the organisation.

Historically, releasing increments of change carried significant overhead. This typically builds up in an organisation over time. Change carries a perceived or actual risk and processes are introduced to counter this. This 'release tax' means releases occur less frequently, become bigger and inherently more risky. As a result the problem is perpetuated. Continuous Delivery and DevOps techniques help organisations break free from this trap.

CONCEPTS

THE PRODUCT INCREMENT

The unit of change is the Product Increment. This is the delta that gets released to users following implementation by the Product Team. A Product Increment may be small and consist of a single simple change or be much larger and contain many changes.

When making a change to a product it is important to consider the full stack of elements required and to release this as a cohesive unit. Implementing the change should involve releasing the technology and supporting manual processes simultaneously.

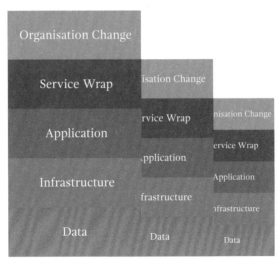

Figure 7-1 : Full Stack Product Increments

A cohesive Product Team will work to ensure that an increment of change to the product is inclusive of all components required to provide value for users and the organisation.

This full stack of change incorporates data, technology (application and infrastructure), service wrap and organisation change. This can be a challenge when the Agile technology delivery meets the non-Agile world of people change, recruitment, training etc. This is where the real breakthrough in organisational Agility can occur. Success here is easier to obtain for digital products and Systems of Engagement than for Systems of Record. Good structured analysis around user needs and a compelling user experience will minimise the need for areas such as user training. The layers of the full stack are explored further below.

ORGANISATION CHANGE LAYER

Deals with the business impact created through updates to the technology components of the product and/or changes to manual, non technology-driven product features such as fulfilment and logistics.

Where a new user Feature is realised in both technology and organisational change, these activities should be aligned in the Product Increment.

SERVICE WRAP LAYER

Defines the supporting people, processes and technology to 'run' the technology product in line with user expectations and agreed service levels.

Changes to the underlying technology infrastructure and application should result in corresponding and fully aligned changes to the supporting processes.

APPLICATION LAYER

The software required to realise the Features of the product that are delivered through technology. Changes here are taken from the prioritised backlog of Features identified through structured analysis.

INFRASTRUCTURE LAYER

The underlying platform on which the application software resides. Rapid Agile change is easier to obtain here when using software-defined infrastructure in some form of Cloud solution.

The underlying configuration management database (CMDB) should evolve incrementally in sync with the application software.

DATA LAYER

Data is a frequently overlooked component of change. It is extremely important that this is considered. Changes to the data model, reference, data, test data and production data must be factored into the change.

Failure to test a change with production data is a common cause of difficulties in getting a technology change to function properly.

Alternative Modes of Operation

There are two common ways of delivering a Product Increment. Firstly each individual change can be considered in isolation and released as required. Secondly several Features, perhaps related under a theme, can be delivered together using a Sprint pattern.

The mode used typically depends on the volume of change, size of team, but more significantly the maturity of the product. Where Feature change is low in a mature product and changes are typically defect related, then these are more likely to be fixed and released without a Sprint pattern. During the development of a MVP, or making significant or several Feature changes a Sprint pattern is more useful.

For the bulk of the work we do we find a Sprint pattern and the associated ceremonies very useful, and in the case of any significant new product development, essential.

Mode	Characteristic	Usage
Sprint Container	Work for each Sprint is planned and estimated up front. Activities around each Sprint to wrap up and feedback on team performance. Typically aligned to the Scrum methodology.	Delivery of several Feature changes or a MVP.
No Container	Work taken as required into delivery teams. Low ceremony based around moving tasks through a small number of discrete phases. Typically aligned to the Kanban methodology.	Delivery of small discrete Feature changes or defects.

Table 7-1 : Pattern Alternatives

BJSS Opinion

Always Use the Process

A key part of the power of Agile is the feedback loop - an ability to fail fast and make many minor course corrections rather than having to deal with a big problem. The Sprint ceremonies we describe in this chapter embody this thinking. The use of the Sprint enables the adoption of lean thinking and a learning loop as illustrated in **Figure 7-2**.

Figure 7-2 : Lean Thinking Learning Loop

It may seem obvious, but to get the benefit of the activities required to plan, monitor and control a Sprint they must be undertaken systematically. All too often when we are engaged in project or programme recovery we see that these basics have slipped in some way, such as:

- Retrospectives are cancelled because the team is too busy

- Incorrect participation in planning sessions

- Show and tell meetings moved out

- Sprints extended

Get into the rhythm of Sprint delivery and stick to it!

THE ENTERPRISE AGILE APPROACH

STARTING AND FINISHING A STORY

We want to be confident that in developing a Product Increment it is complete on delivery and meets quality expectations. To achieve this and run a productive delivery pipeline relies upon understanding what 'Good' looks like both before and after implementing the change.

Commonly used techniques for achieving this include the use of a **Definition of Ready** and a **Definition of Done**. These terms should be defined and communicated in such a way that whole team recognises them and is able to call out any deviations they observe.

Failure to be strong around the implementation of these criteria can easily result in the wrong change being delivered or delivered to a poor level of quality. Never, ever, no matter how tempting, fudge the Definition of Done. Change is not done until it is done! Significant issues will result from watering down the Definition of Done. Transparency over delivery progress will be lost and in our experience the team rarely catches up.

Using a Definition of Ready ensures that requirements, usually expressed as User Stories are completed to a high standard and provide a strong basis for estimating and tracking against. Teams often use the acronym **INVEST** to provide an effective and easy to remember Definition of Ready. This definition may be modified where required provided that all the team sign up to it.

I	Independent	Isolated from other Stories.
N	Negotiable	Will be refined during delivery.
V	Valuable	Adds value to the product and organisation.
E	Estimable	Can be estimated.
S	Small	Will fit into a Sprint.
T	Testable	Has acceptance criteria.

Table 7-2 : INVEST acronym for Definition of Ready

Similarly a Definition of Done is produced in agreement with the team and clearly communicated. Implementing a good Definition of Done can be problematic. This should be an auditable checklist that is sufficiently exhaustive to safeguard delivery and quality without being too unwieldy.

'Done' is often an emotive point. Ultimately a change is not done until it is in the hands of users. This is where some teams find it useful to have multiple layers of Definition of Done that map to the relevant endpoints for particular activities. It is essential to be clear on expectations around Definition of Done with stakeholders. Nobody likes an unpleasant surprise and to be told something is finished when it isn't.

We find it useful to link the Definition of Done back to the V-model. To avoid complexity and ensure proper Agility we believe that there can be no more than three levels of Definition of Done. This is mapped to a simplified V-model in **Figure 7-3**.

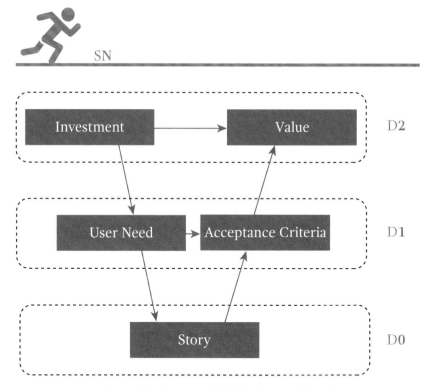

Figure 7-3 : Layering of the 'Definition of Done'

The Definition of Done at each layer corresponds to satisfactorily meeting the criteria a particular group has of the change.

D0 is likely to be more technical in nature and include things the team wishes to achieve to ensure product quality and maintainability. An outline of the layered definitions is provided in **Table 7-3**.

Layer	Done	Typical Definition
D0	To the satisfaction of the Product Team.	The team has completed the delivery of the Story and tested to its satisfaction and updated associated documentation.
D1	To the satisfaction of the specifying user.	The Story has been tested and accepted by the broader organisation and is deemed to meet the acceptance criteria.
D2	Released to the user community.	The Story has been released and is in use across the user community. Value can be generated for the organisation.

Table 7-3 : Layered 'Definition of Done'

SPRINT DELIVERY PATTERNS

The use of Sprints sets the delivery cadence, with Sprint ceremonies taking place at the start, during and at the end of a Sprint. We are often asked about the optimum Sprint length. The team needs time to deliver Stories that are meaningful to the user, but Sprints cannot be too long otherwise the benefits of the process are lost. In our experience, anything longer than four weeks is too long and anything less than a week is too short. Our default position is for two week Sprints.

The objective of any Sprint is to complete the planned User Stories consistent with the Definition of Done. For small scale changes this will often mean that the solution is ready to go into production. For larger scale change initiatives there are likely to be further activities to be concluded in order to wrap up the release and get it into production.

As far as possible the activities to make the Stories delivered in a Sprint ready for live should be undertaken in the Sprint to avoid a Waterfall-style end game. A release will only take place when there is a meaningful Product Increment that adds value, and this may take more than one Sprint to achieve. It can take many Sprints to get to the point of an initial MVP release. In this situation we recommend that the path to live is still automated and rehearsed to avoid back-loaded risk.

Figure 7-4 : Sprint Delivery Pattern

In the example in **Figure 7-4** we have identified a theoretical Sprint delivery pattern in which a Product Increment is released every three Sprints. This pattern identifies the use of two special purpose Sprints - Sprint 0 and the Release Sprint are used to achieve particular aims aside from Feature delivery. Where a release does not occur every Sprint it may be necessary for a Release Sprint to be used to bring together non-Agile work streams and activities such as organisation change, and less Agile technology delivery of back office systems in a multi-modal technology landscape.

USE OF SPECIAL SPRINTS

SPRINT 0

The first Sprint of technology delivery is a special purpose Sprint to prepare the ground for effective delivery in subsequent Sprints. In essence Sprint 0 bootstraps and primes the delivery pipeline. On large-scale change initiatives, earlier phases of risk reduction, such as Discovery may have already built the delivery pipeline in order to produce architectural PoCs. In this case Sprint 0 will focus on making the delivery pipeline production quality and able to scale for use by the full team.

It is useful to build a set of technical stories with acceptance criteria to define the activities of Sprint 0, just as you would for any other Feature Sprint. Whilst the specific technical tasks of a Sprint 0 will vary by product and technology stack, we have identified some key goals of a Sprint 0 below.

1. Agile lifecycle tooling and workflow established.

2. Code quality dashboard and static analysis tools installed and configured.

3. Unit test framework established.

4. Continuous Integration (software build) tooling installed and configured.

5. Engineer code (desktop) environment established.

6. Basic test platform available.

7. Automated deployment script started.

8. Team on-boarding guidance developed (technical and product orientation.)

9. Delivery metrics, collation and reporting established.

10. Technical governance process in place.

RELEASE SPRINTS

A Release Sprint is a special vehicle for wrapping up change and getting it into the hands of users. The aim should always be to deliver production-ready software after each Sprint. There are some occasions where additional activities are required, such as final compliance steps like mobile app store verification, integration with non-Agile work streams or alignment with certain organisational change activities.

In these situations such work can be done in parallel to Feature Sprints, or where the effort required may be considerable, the team can be given time away from Feature delivery to focus on release activity. The use of Release Sprints cannot really be mandated by any particular rules, it is a useful tool to consider when delivering complex products and change across the organisation.

THE PRACTICES OF EFFECTIVE SPRINTS

Day 1 and day 10 of a Sprint will not necessarily be the same. There is a pattern to a Sprint that is required in order to ensure successful high quality delivery of change. Specific activities are required in order to plan, execute, control and wrap up a Sprint.

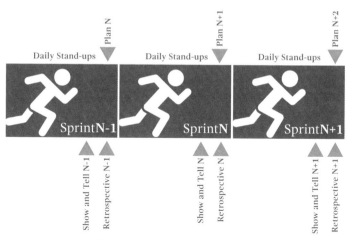

Figure 7-5 : Anatomy of a Sprint

A small number of key activities make a Sprint successful. In our view all are essential to ensure productive high quality delivery and to manage expectations and avoid surprises.

PLANNING

The purpose of the Sprint planning session is to take a set of Stories that meet the Definition of Ready into the next Sprint. These meetings usually include the whole delivery team and the Product Owner. The team works through the prioritised Product Backlog and receives any clarifications on user needs from the Product Owner and Analysts.

A key part of the planning process is estimating the Stories taken in Sprint and decomposing into the relevant tasks. In Chapter 5 we discussed the estimation process used during Discovery. At that stage blind estimation techniques can be useful, however at Sprint planning we recommend consensus-based estimation. Teams may use a form of Agile planning poker to arrive at estimates. Using this method the Story is discussed and each member of the team offers his or her estimate. Sometimes this is done by showing a card, from a set with the Fibonacci sequence numbers on.

The advantage of this estimation technique is that it flushes out unknowns and information that not all team members might have. Not only does it support knowledge transfer across the team, it is also likely to result in better estimates.

Obviously for this session to be effective some work will have to be done in advance by analysts to ensure that the candidate Stories are suitably elaborated to be developed and meet the Definition of Ready. In addition analysts and team leads will be working ahead by one or two Sprints to manage any dependencies with the leadership functions to ensure the Story is independent of others.

Working ahead of the Sprint planning process may also throw up some design work and decisions. Where necessary these should be taken to the design authority prior to Sprint planning. When filling a Sprint with Stories always include capacity for defects and support incidents.

The output of the Sprint planning meeting should include:

1. **The Theme of the Sprint**
   The general topic or areas of change being delivered and the goals of the Sprint.

2. **The Sprint Backlog**
   The set of estimated prioritised Stories for delivery in the Sprint.

3. **Quantifiable Spare Capacity**
   To handle defects and support incidents coming through that need to be addressed by the Sprint.

4. **A Commitment to Deliver**
   All parties involved offer their support for the delivery of the Sprint backlog, this includes external dependencies that may need to be secured by the leadership team.

DAILY STAND-UP

The daily Stand-up is the heartbeat of the Product Team. We believe it applies equally well to delivery and service teams. Each team will run its own Stand-up. In a Product Team of multiple teams, each Team Lead will get together and run a Team Lead Stand-up.

The objectives of the daily Stand-up are to ensure that:

1. The team is updated on what each member is doing.

2. Any blockers are identified and quickly addressed or escalated.

In order to meet these simple objectives the format is kept clear and focused. The team assembles, usually in or close to their regular working environment and take it in turns to briefly inform the team of:

1. What they did yesterday.

2. What they are doing today.

3. Any blockers they are experiencing.

It is the job of the team lead to control the Stand-up and make sure that any debate is taken away and continued outside the meeting. Typically the Stand-up will not take any longer than 10 minutes and is usually best conducted first thing in the morning when the team arrive – after they have made a cup of coffee. They are called Stand-ups for a reason, these sessions should never be conducted seated in a meeting room!

SHOW AND TELL

The Show and Tell is the end of Sprint ceremony for wrapping up the delivery with the key stakeholders. During Sprint planning at the start of the Sprint, all parties will have agreed to what Stories are going to be delivered. The Show and Tell demonstrates those Stories as either working software or other change artefacts.

We believe in establishing clear traceability so the demonstration of work delivered is usually accompanied by a brief presentation or dashboard showing what was committed to during Sprint planning and what has now been delivered along with a summary of any known issues. A simple example of this is illustrated in **Figure 7-6**.

Sprint: 7   **Theme:** Account Management

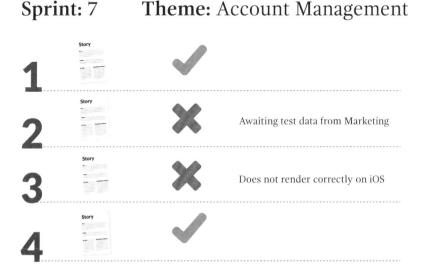

Figure 7-6 : Simple Traceability Report for Show and Tell

Show and Tell meetings are usually held at or just after the end of Sprint, depending on the logistics of getting everyone in a room at the same time. The team should be ready to hold this session by the end of the Sprint. Sometimes it is useful to run the Show and Tell and the planning session for the next Sprint back-to-back at the end of the Sprint.

RETROSPECTIVE

The Retrospective meeting is the Agile feedback loop and is an essential part of the process. It is held within the Product Team and is used to mature the process and iron out wrinkles. The retrospective allows the team to identify what went well and what they would like to change. It also allows persistent issues and challenges to be escalated.

The format of the retrospective is straightforward:

1. The team assembles and the lead sets the context and reminds the team of the format.

2. Everyone writes their Good, Bad and Puzzling observations on Post-it notes.

3. In turn everyone steps up and adds their notes to the wall explaining each point.

4. The notes are grouped into related themes.

5. A set of actions is collated and agreed across the team.

There are many ways of categorising the feedback however we prefer to use three groups, as identified in **Figure 7-7**.

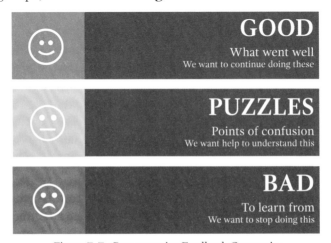

Figure 7-7 : Retrospective Feedback Categories

UPDATING THE SERVICE WRAP

As highlighted at the beginning of this chapter, the broader Product Team working together to deliver a complete Product Increment is essential to achieving organisation Agility. The change released is not just a technology update, but also a corresponding update to the supporting processes.

In Chapter 9 we explore how the delivery pipeline can now automate many of the traditional service functions. That said, it is still necessary to ensure that support teams are familiar with the new functionality and are able to effectively handle incidents raised by users. This work should be quite lightweight. We expect support teams to be working alongside delivery teams as part of the broader Product Team.

Service Teams will have full visibility of change flowing through the delivery pipeline and be included in broader team activities and Sprint ceremonies. The key here is not to treat service as distinct from change and to include Service Teams in the wider Product Team.

COMBINING ORGANISATION AND TECHNOLOGY CHANGE

The Sprint pattern is not just applicable to delivering technology change, it is also suitable for delivering the full Product Increment. Often some non-technological change carries real-world constraints, particularly those around operational logistics and personnel that require legal and contractual input - alignment is required.

Sprint Backlog

Figure 7-8 : Concurrent Technical and Manual Process Delivery

Aligning organisation and technical change starts with clear strategy and objectives. This is essential and feeds the structured analysis work that provides the links between technology and manual processes. The User Journeys produced to describe the required changes will identify what is achieved using technology ('in-system') and what is delivered via manual processes ('out-of-system'). The Agile nature of the delivery means that scope will change and decisions based on value derived by the organisation will refine the in-system versus out-of-system boundary.

We recommend that the organisation change activities required to support new product Features be delivered as part of the same Sprint pattern to minimise a potentially risky rollout of the change. The definition of manual processes and supporting artefacts should be produced at the same time as the related technological change and is often undertaken by a specialist team of analysts.

KEY POINTS

1 Make sure a deliverable Product Increment includes the changes to all aspects of the product stack - business change, service wrap, and technology (application, data and infrastructure).

2 Only take Stories into Sprint that meet the Definition of Ready and only earn value from Stories that meet the Definition of Done.

3 Use a Sprint 0 at the start of the Delivery phase to initiate the delivery pipeline and get all the necessary tooling and automation in place.

4 Ensure every Sprint includes sessions for planning and estimating, daily Stand-ups, Show and Tells and Retrospectives, and that these are never cancelled.

5 Align organisation change and manual process updates to the same Sprint delivery and release cadence where possible.

8

Engineering Quality Outcomes

Technology delivery is a fascinating discipline that combines engineering precision with a creative flair. We believe that the best quality outcomes in terms of technology delivery arise from a structured approach to engineering built around automated, repeatable processes.

The field of software engineering is constantly evolving and recent innovations such as software-defined infrastructure have brought new opportunities and challenges for delivering Agile change. We have long advocated the need to remove back-loaded risk from technology delivery through continuous integration, automated test and deployment.

CONCEPTS

KEY COMPONENTS OF ENGINEERING DELIVERY

The modern engineering landscape as popularised by the term DevOps comprises the three key components illustrated in **Figure 8-1**.

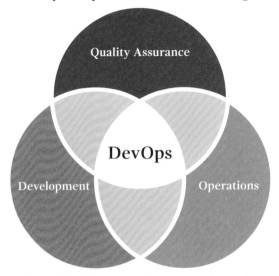

Figure 8-1 : Engineering Components in DevOps

It is important to note that the key enabler to DevOps is good quality assurance through test automation. Bringing together Development and Operations is considered too risky for many organisations, but is essential in order to release change to users often and deliver the wider organisation benefits of greater Agility. Effective QA is the means of managing that risk and making DevOps a reality.

BJSS OPINION

START WITH STRONG ARCHITECTURE

Good engineering starts with strong architecture. For a time during the early days of Agile delivery the term 'Emergent architecture' became fashionable. Coding without architecture isn't Agile delivery, it's hacking - nothing more than a code and fix approach. Whilst this might work for small-scale pieces of work, it is no way to conduct product development in a professional organisation.

Being more Agile doesn't mean allowing the engineering function to become a developer playground with no rules. The consequences of an emergent architecture are a total lack of predictability in delivery. Discovering that you must support 10,000 users after six months of development work, requiring a complete change of the technology stack isn't the kind of problem most organisations can swallow.

In general terms when developing a new product the architecture for the MVP is defined upfront and tested using PoCs and prototypes during Discovery. This provides for a level of predictability and reduced delivery risk during the implementation of the initial product version. Solution architecture is largely impacted by the non-functional requirements of the product, so early emphasis on getting these agreed is important.

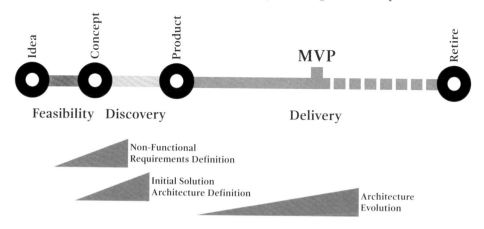

Figure 8-2 : Architecture Definition

It would be naïve to assume that architecture is defined 100% upfront without subsequent modification. The architecture of the product will continue to change as the product changes, particularly post-launch. Updates to the product architecture occur through controlled evolution and not emergence. Significant architectural changes have the capacity to cause widespread disruption to the delivery pipeline if not managed correctly. In extreme cases we have seen this completely halt delivery of functional change.

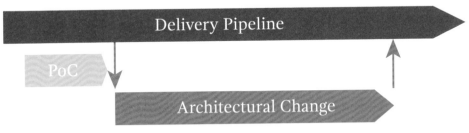

Figure 8-3 : Introducing Architectural Change

The process of making architectural change is a surgical procedure, and is largely the same irrespective of where in the architecture the change is - business, application, data or technology. The change will likely comprise a large-scale code change and a modification to the delivery pipeline. Strong engineering principles executed through good configuration management, source code control and branch and merge policies are essential. The key steps are:

1. Identification of requirement for architectural change leads to a PoC to confirm the approach.

2. Architectural change is undertaken in a separate code branch to avoid impacting normal functional delivery.

3. The change is merged back into the pipeline when complete or ideally periodically where this is feasible.

The most important point is that architectural change is only committed to the delivery pipeline and shippable product when all assurance and tests have been completed. Technical changes should never break the pipeline or impact product quality.

Given the serious problems that technical changes can bring, we recommend always following these rules:

1. There are written requirements and acceptance criteria in the same way as for functional change.

2. Change is only made when it adds value to the organisation, this may be indirect, e.g. improving the efficiency of the team.

3. Implementation is undertaken within the product team, not by architects in isolation.

The last point may seem counter-intuitive, but there will be long term consequences for knowledge and morale if the perceived 'hard' technical work is the preserve of an elite. The product team need to be able to know how to continue to change and run the product.

MEASURE FOR SUCCESS

In order to aid predictable delivery and continuously improve it is essential to put in place the right measures around delivering change and service. We believe that metrics collection and reporting should largely be automated by the lifecycle tooling. It is also important that there is complete transparency over the metrics from the team all the way up to the sponsor.

There is considerable debate amongst the Agile community as to how, and if, teams should be measured. In many ways, excessive measurement is counter to the spirit of Agile development, but in scenarios where large scale change is being delivered, measurement is essential. It is vital to gain the trust of the team by being transparent about what metrics are being collected and what they are used for.

ENGINEERING GOOD CUSTOMER SERVICE

A key component of delivering complete Product Increments is the Service Wrap - the processes and procedures that support the user when experiencing difficulty using the product.

Traditionally the service component of product delivery has been separate from the development efforts to change the product. To be effective at rapid low risk change we believe that 'Build' and 'Run' should be combined. Chapter 9 provides a description of this approach and how Agile and ITiL can co-exist in a single DevOps delivery unit.

THE ENTERPRISE AGILE APPROACH

BUILDING THE DELIVERY PIPELINE

The delivery pipeline - the technology and tooling through which new Product Increments flow - is core to delivering technology change. Establishing the basic delivery pipeline during Sprint 0 is an essential investment. Without it the process of delivering change relies on manual processes and a collection of error-prone and time consuming scripts.

At the heart of the delivery pipeline is an integrated tool chain. These engineering tools should support all aspects of building and running the product. Getting these products up and running from the start of product delivery is strongly recommended, however it is possible to add to existing product delivery where this hasn't been used in the past. On larger scale product teams it is sometimes the case that a specialist team (or individual) looks after tooling. This is a judgment call - we suggest that all engineers should have a good working knowledge of the tooling and how it fits together.

Figure 8-4 : Typical DevOps Tool Chain

Figure 8-4 shows an example of the categories of tools in the end-to-end tool chain to support the delivery pipeline.

OPERATING AND IMPROVING THE DELIVERY PIPELINE

Time should be allowed both pre- and post- product launch to maintain and improve the delivery pipeline. Doing so preserves the efficiency of the team and reduces the risk of failures. Required changes to the pipeline are most likely to originate from the team themselves during their normal Stand-ups and Retrospectives. These changes should be recorded as defects or new Stories and added to the backlog. They are then prioritised and fed into the normal Sprint planning process against reserved maintenance capacity.

If the pipeline becomes faulty then delivery should stop. A big mistake we see teams make is to carry on in this situation. If the continuous integration process or automated tests are not working, the team must halt all feature delivery and concentrate on fixing the problem. Without the correct controls in place there is no knowing what the product quality is. Furthermore if tests are failing then continuing to change and add new areas of untested functionality to the product will compound the problem. If the build breaks, the pipeline is faulty and normal delivery stops – no excuses. Ever!

We expect instrumentation to be applied in production and to the delivery pipeline. Sudden increases in build times, test execution times etc. may point to a problem that will soon impact productivity. Such issues should be recorded and dealt with as potential defects in the same way as product defects. Remember, the delivery pipeline is the vehicle for implementing technology change - it needs maintaining and repairing in order to continue to be successful.

BUILDING IN PRODUCT QUALITY

Product quality is engineered-in throughout the delivery process. It cannot be easily 'tested in' afterwards. This requires a clear approach to testing that ensures potential issues are identified early. It is only through these (largely automated) test activities that a DevOps approach can succeed.

Pushing frequent change through the delivery pipeline and into the hands of the users requires assurance that things aren't going to break. Test activities evolve across the product lifecycle as shown in **Figure 8-5**.

It is important to recognise that everyone is engaged in quality and test activities, and that this is integral to the work of each team. The focus on testing begins at the outset and helps shape the realisation of the initial idea. Early consideration of test activities is essential to the delivery of a quality product. The first areas to consider are how the delivery of the product can be assured and the role that testing plays in this. The initial approach will consider the required test activities, levels of automation, framework, roles, environments and data.

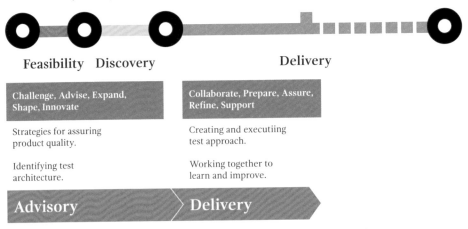

Figure 8-5 : Test Evolution Across the Product Lifecycle

The role of testing is to ensure that a high quality product can be delivered continuously and consistently. This requires attention to four functions:

1. **Test Leadership**
   Advising and guiding the Product Owner and informing the governance process on approaches to quality and potential issues.

2. **Test Architecture**
   Aligning a suitable set of tools and frameworks to the product, assuring quality without creating a cottage industry to maintain bespoke artefacts.

3. **Functional Testing**
   Adding value through knowledge of the product, users and market to ensure needs are met and a quality user experience.

4. **Technical Testing**
   Making sure that the product will cope with the rigours of real-world use and meets the required non-functional requirements.

It is important to note that testing has a role to play in all aspects of the product stack. Don't confine your thinking and test strategy to the application software. Data quality, infrastructure and service all impact the experience of the user.

DEVELOPING A STRATEGY FOR TESTING

Using a test strategy is a powerful way to capture and focus energy on test activities. Exhaustively testing (manual or automated) all aspects of the product following a change is not feasible. The strategy allows for test objectives to be set and achieved and directs effort to where it is most needed based on risk and effectiveness.

Ultimately the aim of testing is to ensure the product can be released to users with a reasonable level of predictability and quality. A good test strategy will include the following key elements:

1. **Test Objectives**
    Shaping the balance of testing methods employed and the focus of the team is derived from clear test objectives. This is likely to reflect the acceptable risk profile and external constraints such as compliance.

2. **Contribution to Governance**
    Product quality is one of the key measures of interest to stakeholders. The output of test activities must be articulated in a crisp and concise manner such that it can inform any required support or interventions.

3. **Information Sharing**
    The entire product team relies on data relating to testing to help focus its efforts, so clarity here is important. Issues arising during testing may point to the need to address skills and capability within the team or resolve design problems.

4. **Test Architecture**
    This may sound a rather grand term, but it is important to consider how test activities interact and overlap. Test architecture will capture the structure of the testing landscape and identify the supporting frameworks and tools required.

5. **Test Method**
    Consideration must be given to how the testing will take place and the execution process, the level of automation and the

underpinning data and environments that will be used. This will help the team plan test tasks and interactions across the organisation.

DETERMINING WHERE TO FOCUS TEST EFFORT

Creating automated tests is a significant investment. Not only does creating the tests require engineering skill and labour, but every product change will require further tests and updates to existing tests. When creating a test strategy and considering where to invest in automation we find the Agile test automation pyramid in **Figure 8-6** useful. This identifies that the bulk of automation effort should be focused on unit tests ahead of service (API) tests and UI automation.

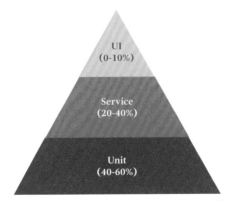

Figure 8-6 : Agile Test Automation Pyramid

This approach offers a number of clear advantages. Firstly it builds quality into the product from within. Traditional test approaches might have a team of people or large automation packs created by testers focused on the interface and not the implementation.

Secondly, relying on big UI automation packs is inefficient - they quickly become brittle and are costly to maintain.

Thirdly, the bias towards unit and service tests pushes the bulk of test automation back into the development space, forcing developers to own product quality which has a general overall positive effect.

It is common to see the pyramid model extended to cover additional test phases and also suggest the level of effort to be expended on manual testing. An example of an enhanced test pyramid is shown in **Figure 8-7**.

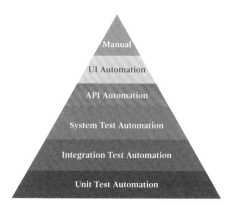

Figure 8-7 : Expanded Agile Test Pyramid

A Structured Approach to Testing

In Chapter 6 we discussed the importance of a structured approach to Analysis. For obvious reasons, validating that layered requirements have been met necessitates a layered approach to testing. This yields consideration for the established V-model. The concept of the V-model was originally coupled to more traditional waterfall projects. However the principle can still apply to an Agile delivery with the 'V' repeated every Sprint (or set of Sprints forming a release). We refer to this as the W-model.

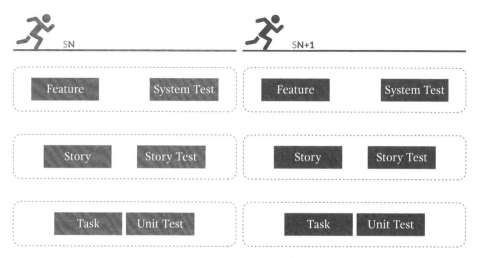

Figure 8-8 : W-Model

In devising the approach to testing the team must consider the balance of requirements-based testing and risk-based testing. Both have a part to play in ensuring product quality. All Stories will be written with acceptance criteria that need to be tested against. Further testing beyond that and into obscure edge cases should be driven by risk.

It is useful (not just from a testing perspective) to know what the most frequent and most valuable transactions in the product are. This information can be used to help prioritise testing efforts.

TEST PHASES AND THE SPRINT PATTERN

We expect that meeting the acceptance criteria defined for each User Story is part of the Definition of Done. This correctly implies that Story acceptance testing will take place during the same Sprint as the Story is developed. Where change is relatively small, it should be possible to conclude all necessary testing during a Sprint. The automated delivery pipeline assures this and uses packs of automated tests to allow software to be deployed into live at the touch of a button.

There are of course valid exceptions to this process. Many of the systems we work with require further manual testing or integration with non-Agile work streams and legacy systems. In such scenarios these test phases may occur in parallel to on-going feature development or during a special purpose Release Sprint. **Figure 8-9** illustrates the test phases we recommend and how this is achieved across the delivery pattern.

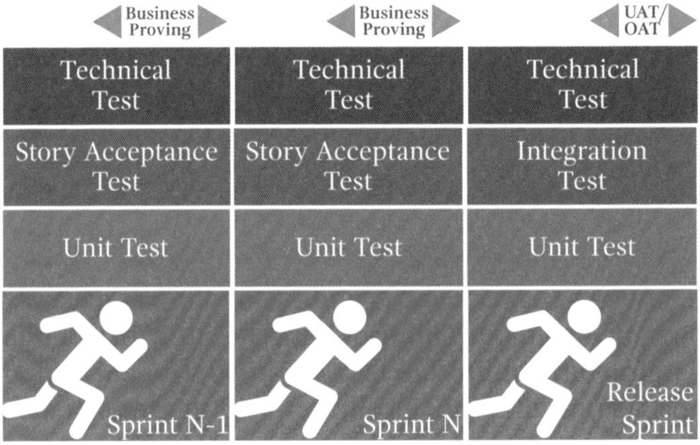

Figure 8-9 : Recommended Test Phases

DEALING WITH DEFECTS

No matter how extensive testing efforts are, defects and support incidents will arise. This should be a matter of routine and a large 'bow wave' of defects must not be allowed to accumulate near a release by watering down the Definition of Done or deferring testing. This is why we recommend as much testing occurs in-Sprint as possible and the full Product Increment is produced such that application, infrastructure and data change are aligned and fully working together.

Defects and support work will be added to the Product Backlog and brought into Sprint through the Sprint planning process and delivered alongside new Stories. It is unlikely that all defects to be fixed in a Sprint are discussed at the planning meeting. A more common approach is to allow for some team capacity to address defects in priority order.

To ensure that defects are properly understood and assigned the correct severity rating, teams should run a regular defect triage meeting with the Product Owner. This session not only ensures that defects are categorised and dealt with correctly, it also allows for the removal of duplicates and identification of trends in particular types of defects.

CODING FOR THE CLOUD

One of the most exciting developments in technology in recent years is the advent of software-defined infrastructure and Cloud computing. As software engineering processes move into the infrastructure space so too does opportunity to innovate and increase Agility and flexibility.

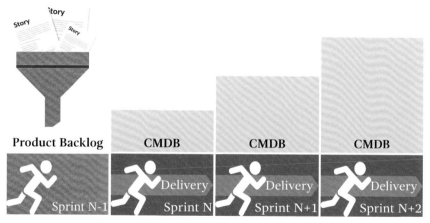

Figure 8-10 : Incremental Infrastructure Delivery

Take for example a requirement to generate a PDF document as an output for a process in the product. The design for this Story might include wrapping a piece of Open Source PDF generation software into a reusable service that is scalable for multiple users and customising some of the functionality. Traditionally, different teams would have undertaken the software customisation and infrastructure work. Now changes to software and infrastructure can flow through the same delivery pipeline. In fact the same engineer could do both pieces of work.

Developing self-contained micro-services with the application and infrastructure technology combined and defined in software allows for infrastructure changes to be delivered incrementally in-Sprint alongside application changes.

The question now arises as to how software-defined infrastructure can be quality assured. The answer is straightforward - use the same automated test techniques used to assure application software. Tools to unit test software-defined infrastructure are a relatively new but emerging field. Completely tearing down and rebuilding the infrastructure (and data) should be an inherent part of the system test cycle.

There are also techniques that should be used to test the deployment of software-defined infrastructure changes. We suggest that such implementations should be validated using inventory scanning tools. A scan before and after can be compared and the delta checked against the specified Configuration Management Database (CMDB) changes to assure that the software correctly implements the required infrastructure.

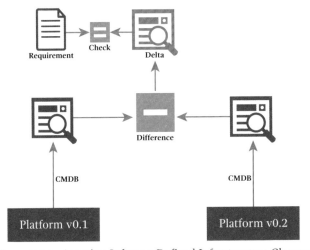

Figure 8-11 : Assuring Software-Defined Infrastructure Changes

DELIVERY AND SERVICE METRICS

If you want to improve something - measure it. We are strong advocates of implementing metrics to understand the performance of the product and the delivery pipeline. In simple terms there are typically three categories of metric that arise from DevOps around a product summarised in **Figure 8-12**.

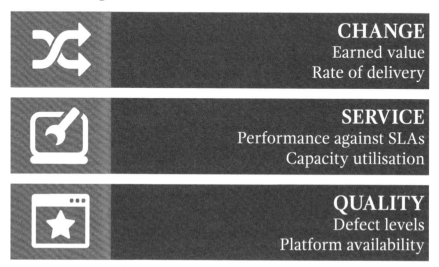

Figure 8-12 : Categories of Product Metrics

The collection and distribution of metrics should be largely automated. We expect this to be part of the end-to-end tool chain. Getting data should not be a chore, but does require a little support across the team. In particular those responsible for delivering change will need to record the actual time spent on tasks and the estimate to complete. This enables the rate of delivery and estimation accuracy to be recorded and used as part of the feedback loop to adjust the forward plan and advise the Sprint planning process.

The ultimate measure for the organisation is earned value and measuring the benefit gained for the effort expended on delivering new features.

Service metrics inform decisions about resource levels in support teams and highlight the quality of service being delivered to users. They also quantify how the platform has been scaling to user needs and the potential cost implications of that scaling.

Measuring product quality is important to ensure that customer expectations continue to be met and product quality remains high. This can be measured by examining defect levels and the stability/availability of the product.

We suggest that a metrics dashboard, transparent and visible to all team members, is produced dynamically from the pipeline tooling.

MEASURING CHANGE

A crucial element of achieving predictability is measuring progress towards the next release and any impediments to this. Many Agile methodologies have devised different ways of achieving this. Measuring velocity (the rate at which work is done) and Burn-down (or Burn-up) charts are common. The challenge is avoiding getting bound up in lots of metrics, while having sufficient information to make decisions and interventions as required. It is also important the metrics tell a story and have appropriate narrative and are not just raw data. Reporting to a senior executive that the team has a velocity of 27 isn't helpful.

Within a Sprint we believe in recording progress using a Burn-down chart. This is because the content of a Sprint should be a fixed scope – the Stories taken into Sprint during the planning session. An example Burn-down chart is provided in **Figure 8-13**. The Burn-down chart should be updated daily as a result of the stand-up and a revised estimate to complete on tasks by engineers.

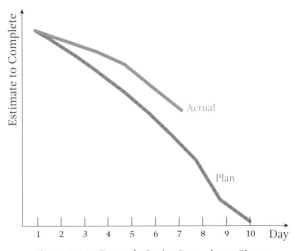

Figure 8-13 : Example Sprint Burn-down Chart

The Burn-down is calculated by plotting the estimate to complete for all the tasks in the Sprint. For tasks in progress this is updated daily by engineers in the delivery team. For tasks not yet started this is the estimate from the Sprint planning session. This actual Burn-down is compared to an ideal trend line that shows all tasks completing by the end of the Sprint. Note that the estimate for complete for a Story should only reach zero when it meets the Definition of Done.

A release may occur after one or more Sprints. For a release we recommend using a Burn-up chart because the scope of a release can change over time as Stories move in or out of the release through the Sprint planning process. As can be seen in **Figure 8-14** the Burn-up release chart clearly identifies a baseline scope for the release. In the case of a MVP this will be the scope agreed during Discovery.

The Burn-up should reflect actual work completed to the Definition of Done. It might be useful to plot the Burn-up for each layer in the Definition of Done to be sure that a gap is not opening up between work completed by the team and being accepted by the user community.

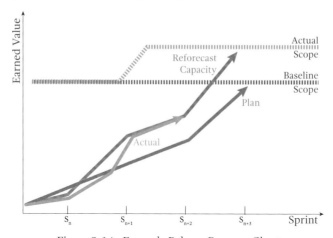

Figure 8-14 : Example Release Burn-up Chart

The concept of earned value is important here. Tracking effort, work done, velocity and so on is useful as an indicator and to aid planning, but most executive sponsors are interested in understanding progress towards goals. If the initiative needs to build 10 widgets to derive value for the organisation, then the only thing that really matters is how many widgets are completed.

In addition to monitoring completed Stories against the baseline we also suggest plotting the actual and planned resource capacity. Inevitably if progress deviates from the expectation then questions will rightly be asked. Often the root cause is simply that less resource was available than expected due to unforeseen holidays and sickness. It is best to make this easily visible such that further analysis into potential issues is only required when the most probable cause of a resource issue is ruled out.

MEASURING SERVICE

Service metrics inform stakeholders about the performance of the product in live use and the level of support being provided. Much of our thinking on service metrics is informed by ITIL processes, combined with the application of a 'Necessary and sufficient' filter. As a minimum service metrics must cover:

1. **Usage of the product by the various user communities.**
    Often this is a non-functional requirement anyway and is certainly important in gaining insight into the interactions of users with the product to inform future enhancements.

2. **Incidents arising from the usage of the system and how the resolution of these performs against any agreed service levels.**
    Incidents will typically be assigned severity levels and the investigation of these may lead to a defect being passed back to the delivery teams.

3. **Capacity that is utilised to deliver the service.**
    This is important for forward planning and financial management and to some extent goes hand in hand with the usage metrics in point 1. These metrics are particularly important when not using elastic Cloud computing platforms.

As with delivery metrics relating to change we would expect these metrics to be largely automated and be derived from the tooling in the delivery pipeline and used by the Service Teams.

MEASURING QUALITY

An important set of metrics are those referring to quality. During the execution of change and service it is important to track the defects found and their path to resolution. We also believe that measuring system availability and unplanned outages is a good indicator of production quality. Many theories and convoluted metrics exist in the area of product quality. We prefer to keep things straightforward and put in place only the 'Necessary and sufficient' metrics.

The number of defects alone does not tell a story or convey any meaningful information. Our recommended key defect metrics are the find and fix rates. These should be plotted over time to provide historical trends. The key question to address is '*Are more defects being found and is resolution keeping pace with discovery?*' Ensuring that a significant gap does not open up between the find and fix rate is key to ensuring a 'No surprises end-game' for the release of a Product Increment.

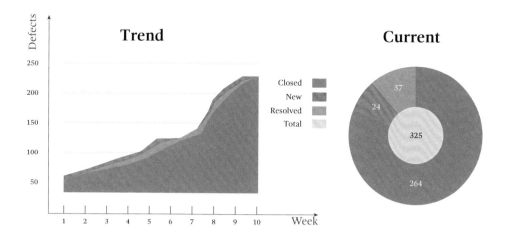

Figure 8-15 : Example Defect Charts

The sample defect charts in **Figure 8-13** illustrate the types of information we expect to see generated automatically from Agile lifecycle tooling and presented transparently for all stakeholders. Data on system availability should similarly be readily producible from the run time tooling in production.

ASSURING TECHNICAL QUALITY

The Architect, with contribution from Technical Leads, will typically develop and implement a Technical Quality Plan (TQP) to underpin the quality of the engineering efforts. The purpose of this TQP is to ensure that all technical output meets the required quality standard. Its scope will include application software, infrastructure (software-defined and hardware), test assets and the full engineering stack.

The TQP should be considered a living artefact that evolves with the product. It is also important to recognise that the document or wiki that represents the TQP is not an end in itself, but a means to an end – high quality technical output. The key areas covered by the TQP are:

1. **Delivery Pipeline Quality**
   The section refers to the use of the delivery pipeline and how to manage the quality of setup and maintenance, including build, continuous integration, packaging and deployment.

2. **Code Quality**
   All aspects of managing the quality of code should be addressed. This will extend to peer code review, static analysis, coding standards, managing technical debt and documentation.

3. **Product Quality**
   This complements the test approach and determines from a technical perspective what 'Good' looks like and how to make effective use of the test tools and frameworks available. Typically this will cover unit test and automated end-to-end tests.

4. **Technical Risk Management**
   Defines a process for identifying and managing technical risks associated with delivering and running the product. This will dovetail into the standard RAID log for overall product delivery.

5. **Knowledge Management**
   An approach is required for capturing, maintaining and sharing technical information relating to the product. This will include, code comments, wikis and traditional documentation.

Do Everything Continuously

Do everything continuously to ensure quality is engineered-in and the risk of delivery failure is low. If you have to do it more than once then automate it and run it regularly. As a minimum, focus on ensuring the following are automated and run continuously:

1. Build.

2. Integration.

3. Functional Tests.

4. Non-functional (Technical) Tests.

5. Data Migration.

6. Deployments.

7. Environment Provisioning.

8. Health monitoring and repair.

KEY POINTS

1 Good engineering starts with strong architecture. Drive out NFRs during Discovery and prove out that architecture early through continuous technical testing.

2 Build and maintain an automated delivery pipeline for the production of high quality software, if the pipeline fails at any point, stop all delivery and fix the problem.

3 Implement a well thought through Test Strategy that identifies the right balance of automation and manual testing, test phases and tooling.

4 Create and use a Technical Quality Plan to manage the code quality process such as code reviews, static analysis, technical debt and associated tooling.

5 Put appropriate tests around software-defined infrastructure and ensure that all software assets are subject to the same source code control.

9

Service Agility

Service management comprises the activities, processes and procedures that an organisation adopts to align IT services with the needs of the business.

We outlined the concept of a Service Wrap in Chapter 8. In this chapter we explore service management concepts in more detail and how organisations can develop and refine a Service Wrap appropriate to their situation. We show how traditional structured approaches can be combined with Agile delivery to provide the level of support required in an Agile delivery pipeline.

Concepts

Service Maturity

Most organisations of any scale operate some type of service function to provide support for products or services. These functions operate at different levels of maturity. A simple service maturity model is shown in **Figure 9-1**.

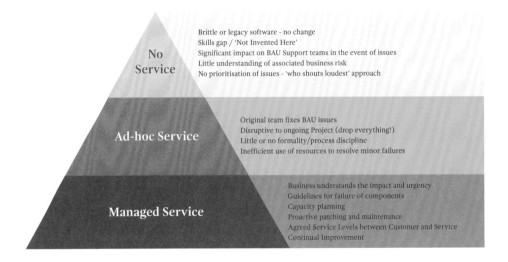

Figure 9-1 : Service Maturity Model

Each maturity level carries a different risk profile and scope to support an agile approach.

No Service

The notion of a product having no service is illusory – if an organisation is using software to conduct elements of its business then a service **is** being provided. Whilst this scenario may seem unlikely in a modern delivery environment, in our experience it is surprisingly common, particularly in the less mainstream areas of a portfolio. It is not uncommon for key production systems to be well defined and managed, whilst other services, perhaps dependencies of that key system, are largely ignored. As a result 'No service' services may be responsible for significant business risk.

A legacy system may be in constant use, and have experienced no issues for long periods of time. Nevertheless a failure would have significant consequences. A common scenario we see is a small number of people managing high value transactions using extremely complex spreadsheet solutions. In many cases these solutions, now operating as key services within the business, have been created by SME staff who have long since moved on. A faulty formula, a regulatory or business change, unforeseen circumstances in the data or technical changes to an unseen dependency can have significant impact (real or reported).

AD-HOC SERVICES

In an Ad-hoc services approach the delivery organisation recognises that a service is being provided, but the ways of working are poorly defined.

A common scenario is that of a project never quite closing down - an otherwise well-managed and well-defined delivery project with poorly defined or non-existent terms of reference for the production system. This often means that the original engineering team that built the solution (the people best placed to support it) remains responsible for resolving any issues, even after the project has disbanded.

This approach works well in mitigating risk, particularly in the early stages of a new service, but it must be a conscious strategy, managed carefully.

It's often the case that the engineers able to support the new service are planned into their next delivery. Diverting them to address 2nd and 3rd line support issues, which usually attract higher priority than project delivery, is disruptive. This unplanned competition for resources creates barriers between teams, friction between colleagues and demotivates the people involved.

Despite these issues, small engineering teams with clear delineation of responsibility and an 'eyes open' approach to planning and estimation can operate this model quite successfully. It is often effective where there is a single point of responsibility which can address any intra-team tensions. For example a single Delivery Manager responsible for Service A and Project B can set direction between the two without recourse to committee decision-making.

Operating a service like this at scale is more difficult. Services of this type tend to over-emphasise the team's project domain knowledge, which naturally erodes over time as the team evolves due to attrition or reorganisation. This approach can breed single points of failure, allowing key person dependencies within the project to extend to the service regime.

Managed Service

Mature service organisations typically employ a service management framework of some kind. A number of standards and frameworks exist, including the Information Technology Infrastructure Library (ITIL), the international standard ISO/IEC 20000, the IT governance framework Control Objectives for Information and related Technologies (COBIT) and elements of The Open Group Architecture Framework (TOGAF).

The most widely used service management framework is ITIL, first developed in the 1980s by the CCTA. The concepts are split into a number of core areas as summarised in **Figure 9-2**.

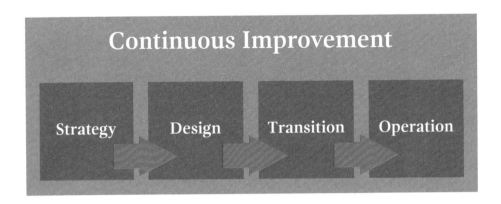

Figure 9-2 : Service Management concepts in ITIL

IT Service Management best practice are the activities, processes and procedures that an organisation adopts to align IT services with the needs of the business. The key elements are:

SERVICE STRATEGY

Service Strategy includes, but isn't limited to, Service Portfolio management, Financial management for IT Services, Demand Management and Business Relationship Management.

SERVICE DESIGN

Service Design considers Service Catalogue Management, Service Level Management, Availability Management, Capacity Management, IT Service Continuity Management, Security Management and Supplier Management.

Using these broad concepts as dimensions, comprehensive service processes can be designed (including supporting procedures), dependencies can be understood and a Service Design can be developed and communicated.

SERVICE TRANSITION

Service Transition covers not only the transition of new services in to a production setting but also ongoing changes to the live service including release and deployment good practice. It includes Transition Planning and Support, Change, Service Asset and Configuration Management, Release and Deployment Management, Service Validation and Testing, Change Evaluation, and Knowledge Management.

SERVICE OPERATION

Service Operation covers the areas familiar to most organisations because these processes and functions are the ones they work with every day. These include Service Desk, Technical Management Application Management and IT Operations Management. Service Operation also covers the processes that deal with Event, Access, Request Fulfilment, Incident and Problem Management.

CONTINUAL SERVICE IMPROVEMENT

The final, overarching core area is Continual Service Improvement. This is an important aspect of any service management approach and ITIL's version covers, amongst other things, a seven step improvement process to enable a service to change with the evolving needs of the business.

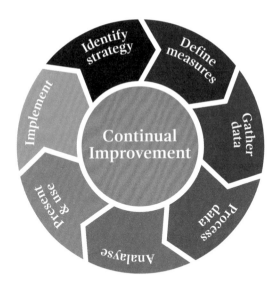

Figure 9-3 : ITIL's Continual Service Improvement approach

Like any framework, ITIL has strengths and weaknesses but it is important to understand the basics. Many books have been written on the various versions of ITIL and we don't propose to duplicate them here. However, the concepts are key to any structured approach to service management.

BJSS OPINION

A structured Service Management approach is sometimes seen by those who don't understand it as a hindrance in Agile environments. Often it is perceived to be an unforgiving, unbending process. This is usually because the details of the service design are not 'fit for purpose'. Many organisations implement what they believe to be best practice but do not take into account the needs of the organisation or speed of change to which it aspires. Note that the design may well have been 'fit for purpose' at the stage it was put in place, but evolving business needs have not been reflected or considered over time.

Service management should be at the heart of an Agile delivery from the outset. It is unlikely that the Service representative will shape the product, but they can advise on potential Service options that influence decision making, before requirements are finalised.

Service design will be heavily influenced by the organisation's appetite for automation. If automation and quality are built in as part of the development of the product and infrastructure, Service processes can be more lightweight, and speed of delivery enhanced.

As with any other Agile process, once service processes are agreed and implemented, they should be refined and reviewed continually. What is relevant in an early life support stage may be irrelevant when the product has proved itself to be stable and resilient. For example, as confidence in the automation grows, along with Service maturity, what would once be counted as a change requiring Change Advisory Board approval, will become a standard change and be pre-approved.

A common misconception is that all best practice Service Management processes should be in place at go live. In practice this depends on the type of project and any external factors. In some circumstances it may be appropriate to design a Minimum Viable Service (MVS) that includes only:

- Incident Management
- Change Management
- Release Management
- Event Management

Other processes can be implemented while the product is live and designed and enhanced in parallel to the product development.

Meeting the challenge

Delivering an effective service is not straightforward. Challenges include:

- Complex, evolving IT estates with multiple component parts

- Aging technical infrastructure and legacy applications

- Legacy or niche technologies, making it difficult (expensive!) to retain skilled staff

- No agreed service levels (Operational Level Agreements) with internal team or between teams

- No journey / plan to modernisation - service designed to 'keep the lights on'

- IT services failing to meet the need of the organisation

In our experience these obstacles can exist even in organisations with a mature approach to service delivery and a clear understanding of their end goal.

Improvements can always be made, regardless of where an organisation fits on the maturity scale. An agile approach will help with an incremental migration to a more mature approach.

Engineering Good Customer Service

ITIL processes typically dominate the service space, and whilst we believe ITIL is still relevant, modern engineering techniques built on software-defined infrastructure and Cloud computing should be used to automate many of these processes, as outlined below.

Service Design

ITIL Process	Automation Solution
Service Catalogue Management	It is likely that the product can automatically register its services in order to maintain a catalogue.
Service Level Management	The Agile DevOps delivery process described throughout this book includes this process.

ITIL Process	Automation Solution
Capacity Management	Whilst it is useful to understand underlying platform constraints and costs, we would expect the delivered product to automatically scale network, compute and storage as required using Cloud technologies.
Availability Management	Using scalable micro-services, automated provisioning, monitoring and self-healing should allow for a product to be almost always available. The use of automated techniques largely reduces the need for manual approaches.
Service Continuity Management	Disaster recovery and service continuity is designed by the Solution Architect during Discovery and should be fully automated within the product delivery.
Information Security Management	A secure coding lifecycle should be adopted to ensure compliance with information security standards.
Supplier Management	Looking after the commercial interests of the organisation and ensuring that suppliers are aligned to goals is a required function of the Product Team.

SERVICE TRANSITION

ITIL Process	Automation Solution
Knowledge Management	Product information should be maintained by the team as part of the on-going service of the product.
Change Management	The rollout of change is completely automated, as is the generation of information allowing complete traceability of the contents of the change. It is likely in most organisations that a developer check-in will not automatically deploy to live and that a final manual Go/No-go decision is made by the CAB.
Asset & Configuration Management	When using software-defined infrastructure, the CMDB can be automatically generated by inventory scanning tools. All configuration, infrastructure and application, should be stored centrally in the source code control repository.

ITIL Process	Automation Solution
Release & Deployment	It is expected that the release and deployment process is fully automated by the delivery pipeline.
	This removes one of the biggest headaches of implementing change where often manual error-prone steps are used to install software products.
Transition Planning	In a large change such as the implementation of a new product some manual transition planning work is still required.
Service Validation & Testing	A suite of automated tests should be used to ensure that the product operates effectively and that automated health checks and healing services operate correctly.
	Some work will be required to check the results of this process and align any remaining manual tests.
Evaluation	The process evaluation category is still potentially useful. We would expect the service to mature through the Agile change process outlined in this book.
	This will be supplemented by audits of the remaining manual processes.

SERVICE OPERATIONS

ITIL Process	Automation Solution
Incident Management	Incident management and dealing with end users will still require human intervention. The investment in an approach to meeting user needs and user-centred design will mean that user queries are reduced.
	Furthermore the focus on automated testing and self-healing infrastructure should mean that reported failures also decline as product reliability increases.
Problem Management	Problem management will still require work from the support teams. These are the challenges that go beyond the automated repair mechanisms of the product.

ITIL Process	Automation Solution
Event Management	The end-to-end tool chain will include operational tools to monitor the health of the product. Events such as low free storage or node failures can be automatically fixed by a self-healing platform and automatically reported to the incident management tool.
Request Fulfilment	By using software-defined infrastructure in the Cloud engineers can self provision the required infrastructure. Little manual work is required, but someone needs to keep an eye on the finances!
Access Management	It is likely that this security-enforcing function remains manual.

CONTINUAL SERVICE IMPROVEMENT

ITIL Process	Automation Solution
Service Measurement	It is recommend that service metrics are automatically generated by the platform.
Service Reporting	Service reporting can largely be automated, however human interpretation of the reports is required to determine any intervention required.
Service Improvement	The service improvement step is still usefully a manual process, but should be tied into the Sprint ceremonies.

ENTERPRISE AGILE APPROACH

Implementing a Service Wrap is key to realising the benefits of good Service Management practice. The Enterprise Agile approach to delivering the Service Wrap is straightforward – treat it as a product to be delivered like any other.

SERVICE AGILITY AT 10,000 FEET

The Enterprise Agile approach to Service Management embraces a DevOps philosophy. Continuous Delivery and cross-functional ways of working are key to delivering agility in the Service Wrap. This way of working breaks the traditional 'Build' and 'Run' ways of thinking.

Figure 9-4 shows the traditional approach to Service Management, based on a 'complete' product being handed over to an Operations organisation to run the service. Future changes are bundled up into a notional 'Release 2' or series of releases.

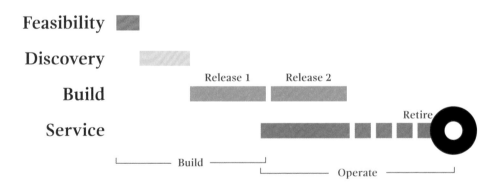

Figure 9-4 : Traditional Service Model

But how does this approach work with a Minimum Viable Product (MVP)? What if the MVP has limited scope and could be earning value for the organisation very quickly, despite substantially more functionality remaining in the Product Backlog? The project is not finished, but the Product must be run. **Figure 9-5** illustrates the Enterprise Agile service model.

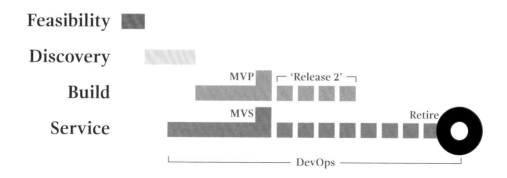

Figure 9-5 : Enterprise Agile Service Model

As soon as the MVP is launched into production, a service is being provided or value cannot be earned. This has a number of implications for the delivery. Service must be considered up front, with a 'Necessary and sufficient' Service Wrap in place. The key point here is Necessary and Sufficient – just as a Minimum Viable Product implements a subset of the Product Backlog, a Minimum Viable Service (MVS) approach can implement an appropriate subset of the Service Wrap.

Thinking about the core concepts, expected usage and ways of working for the MVP helps inform the MVS. In particular, do not underestimate the challenge of managing a team to provide a production quality Managed Service in parallel with delivery of the next wave of features from the product backlog.

Embracing automation as part of the delivery of the MVP, and considering this as part of the strategy and design of the Service Wrap from Discovery onwards provides the right platform for agility in the service. The concept of 'Release 2' becomes irrelevant when changes to the product – and associated service – can be delivered on a Sprint by Sprint basis.

We believe that wherever possible the teams that build an MVP should provide the MVS. Using a DevOps way of working completely removes the 'us and them' of traditional Build and Run teams.

ANATOMY OF A SERVICE WRAP

The Enterprise Agile Service Wrap is a structured approach to good industry practice, drawing on ITIL, with agility at its core.

The Service Wrap provides the people, skills, process and tooling required to allow the MVP and subsequent Product Increments to earn business value.

A Service Wrap typically comprises a number of key capabilities: Platform, Application Support and Maintenance, and New Business Services. The mix will vary for each Service Wrap depending on the unique needs of the underlying Product.

A basic Service Wrap is illustrated in **Figure 9-6**.

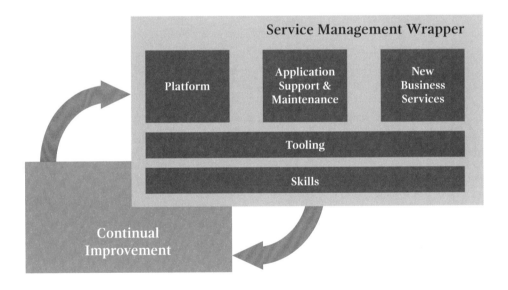

Figure 9-6 : Enterprise Agile Service Wrap

The Service Wrap is based on the following key elements:

- **Service Management Wrapper**
  The fundamental processes that manage the service using an appropriate supporting tool chain, initially implementing the MVS and growing as required. The Managed Service Wrapper is based on a set of appropriate processes implemented by

qualified Service Delivery Managers, Service Support and Process Analysts and specialist teams.

- **Platform**
The Service Wrap must manage the underlying infrastructure of the Product. This may be physical 'tin' on premises or in data centres, or Cloud-based infrastructure. Platform Engineering specialists will be required to deliver the Service Wrap. Platform as a Service (PaaS), Software as a Service (SaaS) and Infrastructure as a Service (IaaS) components may all be relevant depending on the Product.

- **Application Support and Maintenance**
By definition an IT Service is delivered by an existing application stack. Often the technology is dated and technologists will lose interest when supporting it, leading to staff retention issues. This application will require support, together with any required changes and new product implementations. The Service Wrap should ensure that the Product can deliver value to the business. Incidents will arise, issues will be identified and improvements will be required, all of which may impact the value earned. Incident and problem management processes are required supported by resources to resolve any application issues that arise. It's worth considering the backlog of technical debt alongside user-driven support and maintenance items. Constant tactical solutions and 'quick fixes' may introduce Technical Debt and erode quality if not managed carefully.

- **New Business Services**
The Service Wrap isn't just about keeping the infrastructure and application lights on. Product delivery doesn't stop with the MVP. Each Product Increment will transform the service in some way and this must be supported by an appropriate change management approach. Some change will modify existing services, whilst others with introduce Service Wraps of their own. This area is often where new technology is introduced, providing challenges for staff.

Each aspect of the Service Wrap has Continuous Improvement at its core. Regular Service Wrap retrospectives will help identify gaps and areas for improvement, creating new backlog items to enhance and improve the MVS.

There is much more to the Service Wrap than process and tooling alone. As with any Agile transformation there is a Culture and Values dimension. Having the right people, with the right skills and the right mindset is fundamental.

ESTABLISHING THE SERVICE WRAP

The Enterprise Agile method provides a repeatable pattern for delivery that can be specialised to help navigate creation and implementation of the Service Wrap, by treating it as a Product like any other.

The specialised pattern is defined in Figure 9-7.

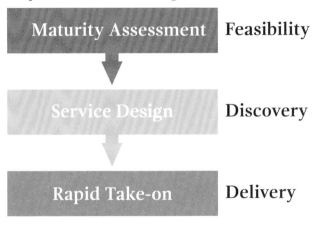

Figure 9-7 : MVS Delivery Pattern

Each step should deliver value to the business:

Maturity Assessment – take stock of the 'as-is' service. Undertake a 'state of the nation' review to understand what is currently in place, what works, what doesn't and where the pain points are.

Service Design – formulate a Process Backlog for the target Service to address the gaps identified by the maturity assessment. Prioritise the backlog into an MVS view, identify any quick wins and establish a plan for delivering the MVS. Identify key Delivery risks and prioritise to achieve the 'No Surprises End Game.'

Rapid Take-On – implement the plan to deliver the MVS, including any knowledge transfer required and establishing any tooling. Refine the Process Backlog as you progress and capture lessons learned during the Delivery.

This not an academic or box ticking exercise. Each Service Wrap will have characteristics unique to the organisation. Identify the target Service Wrap, understand the appropriate MVS for the product and organisation and then apply the pattern to implement it. Consider the Service Wrap from the outset of product delivery and work toward the MVS in readiness for launching the MVP.

Don't try to 'boil the ocean'. Assess what is currently in place, understand the key areas of risk and build a plan to address them with the MVS. Continue to review the Service's Product Backlog and build Continuous Improvement into the way of working right from the start.

1 The Service Wrap should not be a blocker to product development or speed of delivery but can be used as a control mechanism.

2 The Service Wrap should account for the ambitions of the organisation. If the perception is that it is a blocker it should be re-evaluated and updated.

3 Don't try and boil the ocean. Assess what you have, identify the key risks and issues and develop a plan to address them. Review frequently.

4 Continual Service Improvement should be embraced and embedded into the organisation's ways of working.

5 An effective Service Wrap isn't just about process. Ensure the right tools and skilled team members are in place to support it.

10

Making It Work

Many times we have been asked 'How do we become Agile?' The trick to understanding Agility is to move from believing it is a target state, to understanding that it is a journey and a way of being. This may sound a little hippy but it is a key point - achieving greater organisational Agility can only come by adjusting thinking and embedding this into the culture.

The organisation needs to be clear about the intentions behind embracing greater Agility and open with all parties concerned. It should be recognised that this is a long-term commitment and that all benefits will not be realised overnight. We strongly believe in a heavy dose of pragmatism around Agility, try things and fail fast, do not get dogmatic about slavishly following new ways of working that are not right for the organisation.

BJSS Opinion

A Culture of Innovation and Continuous Improvement

Teams will only embark on the transition to a more Agile mind-set if the organisation's culture and values are supportive. Individuals and teams need to be empowered to innovate and try new things in an environment that allows them to 'fail' occasionally. Without some experimentation the organisation will stagnate and decline. Ideas do not only come from the top, innovation most often occurs out in the field within teams who want to improve the way they operate to better service their customers.

The organisation must create, communicate and reinforce what the important values are and allow them to guide behaviour. As we have discussed, the organisation will set some parameters to guide delivery, such as Enterprise Architecture. These centrally controlled functions should be fairly light touch and just sufficient to get the job done.

Bringing Everything Together

Successfully delivering change relies on the alignment of a number of components. We have described the various elements we consider important and offered our views on what does and does not work, based on practical experience.

The model for successful delivery incorporates many things aligned to people, process and technology platform. The key point is that to achieve rapid low risk change, all parties must focus on common objectives. Core to achieving this alignment is determining how to decompose the problem space and get work done.

In our experience, difficulties arise when three central dimensions are cut differently:

1. People organisation and delivery model.
2. Solution architecture.
3. Supplier contracts.

If these areas do not align, delivery becomes troublesome. Getting the team, technology and supplier incentives synchronised allows change to be implemented efficiently with less risk of divergence from the organisation's goals.

USE APPROPRIATE COMMERCIAL MODELS

The need to align all suppliers to a common organisational goal to foster collaboration raises an interesting point around contracts. It is usually the case that supplier contracts are focused around the things that could go wrong rather than aligning everything required for success. That is not to say that it is not important to consider a contract exit and mechanisms for handling poor performance, but we hope these are secondary to getting in place the things required for success.

Most people generally want to do the right thing as an employee. Whilst they come to work to earn money in the absence of other distorting factors, they usually want to build their skills and do a good job. The same is true of most suppliers. In our experience, whilst suppliers want to make a profit they also care about repeat business, their brand reputation and the long-term relationship.

It is likely that an organisation will justifiably want to ensure it gets good value from its suppliers. Various mechanisms exist to try and incentivise suppliers to deliver and behave in the right way. The substantive point is that incentives are used to drive behaviours - make sure you pick the right incentives. We have seen examples where this has gone awry. In one situation a software partner was measured by the number of lines of code it delivered!

THE ENTERPRISE AGILE APPROACH

ADOPTING AGILITY IN THE ORGANISATION

Greater Agility is generally not achieved through training courses and implementing a new target-operating model. We recommend that teams and organisations take an Agile approach to becoming more Agile. Some organisations try and implement a 'sheep dip' conversion process only to arrive back in the office the week after the training course confused as to where to begin.

Plan the Agile journey in the same way as we have described for product delivery. Outline a set of goals for the organisation, develop a roadmap and then progressively move towards achieving these goals incrementally using a Sprint pattern. A big bang transformation of the entire organisation is unlikely to be successful. The only time we advocate starting out with a fully Agile model in mind is a greenfield scenario, for example, when bringing in house a previously outsourced service or launching a brand new product.

A suggested journey to Agility may look something like:

1. Identify drivers for change and articulate these as organisation goals.

2. Create a roadmap for key initiatives and desired value.

3. Find an owner to lead the change, and ambassadors to support them.

4. Develop the core processes and tools to support the transition.

5. Implement across a small number of exemplar products.

6. Constantly review and refine the approach using feedback for each increment.

7. Adjust the roadmap based on lessons learned from early adopters.

8. Broaden the scope to further products across the organisation.

A balance must be struck between creating empowered Agile teams and retaining sufficient central control and alignment to the broader organisation goals. This is where the appropriate governance structures are important - apply the same governance to your Agile journey as you would to running individual product lines.

Another key challenge can be ownership of this drive for Agility. Historically, software delivery teams were the early creators and adopters of Agile techniques. Whilst your organisation should leverage this experience if it exists, there must be executive sponsorship for a wider rollout. If your organisation is structured around functional silos then you need to find a way to bridge this gap. Achieving the real benefits of Agility requires organisations to look beyond the IT department. Executive sponsorship may come from the CEO or CDO.

In practical terms the organisation is likely to need some focused expertise to guide early exemplar projects through the process. For large organisations, having a lightweight central group to develop and promote Agile techniques may be useful. Care must be taken not to develop a central function that mandates new ways of working without some consultation. A 'Centre of Excellence' may be developed that becomes the central repository for knowledge and expertise but operates in a highly collaborative way with product teams.

In summary, there isn't a 'project' to become Agile. Identify goals, produce a roadmap and provide support to teams to help them achieve those goals. The journey to Agile requires on-going support rather than formal training - identify individuals able to coach teams and help them to develop their skills.

Monitor Maturity

A useful tool to identify the progress being made on the Agile journey is the use of maturity models. Expect different product teams to be at different levels of maturity - each team and product is different and the rate of progression will differ, often due to real world external constraints. A maturity model can help highlight which teams need additional coaching or support.

Keep the model simple and supportive. Detailed audits are likely to create concern and are not necessary in an ability-led organisation where experienced Agile leaders are working with product teams. A typical Agile maturity model might include:

1. A series of assessments aligned to the different aspects of Agile product delivery (e.g. define, develop, assure, deploy, operate.)

2. A basic rating mechanism identifying maturity against each category.

3. A method of positioning the different aspects of the product team's work on a maturity scale.

4. A set of prioritised recommendations to take the team to the next stage of maturity.

An example of a maturity assessment against one particular category is illustrated in **Figure 10-1**.

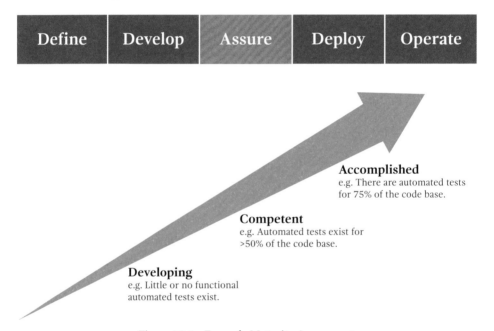

Figure 10-1 : Example Maturity Assessment

FOSTER SUPPLIER COLLABORATION

A key organisational and political element to achieving more rapid change and Agility is to ensure that all barriers are removed - no operational silos exist and all contributing parties are aligned to the same goal.

Meeting this challenge is often why the organisations spearheading Agility are technology start-ups. These organisations have the advantage of no legacy systems and processes and the brand (and finances) to attract and retain the skilled resources they need.

Most organisations do not retain all of the skills they need in house and need to augment their numbers and capability through the use of external suppliers. Getting this relationship right requires effort. Long-term partnerships undoubtedly achieve more than a revolving door of different suppliers. The closer you get to making suppliers an extension of your own organisation and motivated around common goals the more likely you are to achieve results. This suggests a more collaborative approach than traditional procurement-driven relationships.

Contracting for Success

A number of factors play into the contractual arrangement with delivery partners. The organisation would like to incentivise all suppliers around its goals. Such outcome-based arrangements can be hard to broker. The risk is often too high for the supplier to accept and quite reasonably they do not want their profitability to become dependant on the performance of the client organisation and other suppliers.

Four elements require measurement and control:

1. **Delivery** – Have the required outputs been produced?

2. **Quality** – Are the outputs delivered to the required standard?

3. **Citizenship** – Has the supplier worked collaboratively with the organisation and other suppliers?

4. **Cost** - Have all the objectives been met in a cost-effective way?

Ultimately the client organisation needs everyone to cooperate to deliver the services required to the appropriate quality standard. A number of models can be used to drive the required behaviours and achieve the results. These exist on a spectrum from time and materials to fixed price. All models have pros and cons as outlined in **Table 10-1**.

Model	Characteristics	Advantages	Disadvantages
Time and Materials	Supplier invoices for all work done.	Simple to administer.	Supplier not incentivised to deliver to budget.

Model	Characteristics	Advantages	Disadvantages
Target Pricing	Both parties agree a price and overrun is charged at a reduced rate.	An element of risk transfer to the supplier. Maintains focus on outcomes.	Requires both parties to agree a price upfront.
Iterative Delivery	Payments are based around incremental delivery.	Flexibility to fit around Agile delivery. Penalty / bonus agreed Sprint-by-Sprint.	Assumes all the parts make the whole. Risk of focusing on iteration incentive vs final outcome.
Service Levels	A service fee that includes a bonus or penalties based on performance against SLA.	Requires a service that can be defined and measured.	Can miss broader organisation goals and outcomes.
Productivity Based	Supplier is rewarded based on items produced.	Assumes a price can be set for a unit of delivery.	No universally recognised sizing unit that is easy to implement.
Fixed Price	Both parties agree a firm price for the deliverables.	Notionally transfers risk from client to supplier.	A premium for risk transfer. Requires clear upfront scope definition. Change control challenges.

Table 10-1 : Commercial Models

None of these models is perfect for both parties. In our view the best experience is achieved when penalties and incentives are fair and balanced and based on straightforward performance measures. Ideally client and supplier will consider supplier contribution as an on-going activity without constantly referring to the contract. Having vendor management conversations independent of delivery only serves to frustrate the teams.

KEY POINTS

1 Adopting Agile requires a mind-set shift to embrace innovation, continuous improvement and an ability to allow fast failure.

2 Success with Agility can only be achieved when the Delivery Model, Vendor Model and Architecture are aligned and everyone is working towards common goals.

3 Adopting Agile is itself an Agile process, not a big bang transformation - start small, learn, feedback and scale out.

4 Use a lightweight audit process and maturity model to assess where you are on the journey to Agility and monitor successes.

5 When contracting suppliers be sure to align any incentives and penalties with organisation and product delivery goals.

11

Afterword

BJSS Enterprise Agile is based on over 20 years experience of delivering and supporting business critical systems. We employ the approach in our own development centres, and have helped many public and private sector clients to adopt Enterprise Agile to improve the delivery of change initiatives within their organisations.

We hope that you found the concepts and approach we presented here useful. If you would like to begin your journey towards greater Agility then you can begin by accessing further information on BJSS Enterprise Agile online at

bjss.com/ea

Engineering Successful Change

We are often asked about the common pitfalls and lessons learned from running the hundreds of projects that we have undertaken over the last 20 years. In our experience the likelihood of enjoying a 'No surprises end-game' is dramatically improved by following these golden rules:

1. Use a Product Lifecycle to define a pattern to de-risk delivery. Use Feasibility, Discovery and Delivery phases to provide a 'ready, aim, fire' approach.

2. Implement structured and layered analysis to ensure that user needs always relate back to a business outcome.

3. Account for all user needs and define non-functional requirements, including operational requirements during the Discovery phase.

4. Employ routine Sprint ceremonies to plan, monitor and control delivery. Always use Planning, Stand-up, Show and Tell and Retrospective sessions. Never delay or cancel them.

5. Only take Stories into Sprint that meet the Definition of Ready. Stories are only counted as complete when they meet the Definition of Done.

6. Ensure that Analysis, Development and Test are organised as cohesive teams working at the same rate towards common goals. Never allow these activities to become separated or any one of them to fall behind or out of sync with the others.

7. Prove Architecture early by using technical testing that can be automated and repeated continuously throughout delivery.

8. Build a fully automated delivery pipeline during Sprint 0 that includes tooling for development and deployment. If any part of the pipeline breaks, the production of software should stop until it is fixed. Never, for example, work around a failing build by ignoring tests.

9. Attend to data migration early and always test with migrated production data throughout delivery. Only in cases where this is not possible due to security reasons, use synthetic or anonymised data which must still be production-like.

10. Create a transparent, 'visible to all', metrics dashboard that is fed automatically by the delivery pipeline tooling. Ensure that progress and quality are measured.

B

Glossary

Term	Definition
Agile	A set of guiding principles for undertaking the delivery of (software) change.
BDA	Business Design Authority - a body that determines the best route forward for function design decisions. It may be part of a generic Design Authority function.
Bi-modal IT	A model for separating slow changing Systems of Record from faster changing and more Agile Systems of Engagement.
Capability	A logical grouping of individual with the same role taken from several teams.
Cloud	Flexible compute, storage and network capability that may be configured as software using defined APIs.

Term	Definition
CMDB	An inventory log of all the components parts of the underlying technology platform on which the product runs.
Cohort	A group of related users who undertake similar tasks using the product.
Community	A community is an interest group across a large product team or organisation that look at ways to share knowledge and improve ways of working in a particular technology or business domain.
Continuous Delivery	The process of technical automation for software build and deployment.
DA	Design Authority - makes decisions on the functional and technical options for realising change.
Delivery	The phase of the Enterprise Agile product lifecycle that continuously deliver change and service of a product.
Delivery Manager	The individual who works as part of the product leadership function and is responsible for the delivery of change and service for the product.
Delivery Team	A group of individuals working towards a common goal and implementing change.
DevOps	The convergence of software development and technical operations. A key third component that enables this is effective (automated) QA.
Discovery	An intensive risk reduction phase in the Enterprise Agile product lifecycle used to establish a feature backlog for MVP, prove solution architecture, refine the delivery approach and establish assurance and governance controls.
Epic	A group of related User Stories.
Feasibility	The first phase of the Enterprise Agile product lifecycle used to establish goals and objectives.

Term	Definition
Feature	A coarse grained functional requirement that performs a major step in a user journey. Features are decomposed into Epics and Stories.
Full stack engineer	A technologist who undertakes the full range of engineering tasks required to deliver change.
Incremental Delivery	The process of delivering change in discrete chunks.
Innovation Lab	The combination of lean thinking, a process and behaviours to generate new ideas for products.
ITIL	The Information Technology Information Library - a standard set of processes for Service Management.
Kanban	A lean process for the delivery of change based on work in progress limits.
KDD	Key Design Decision log - used to record the output of a design authority process.
Lean	A process philosophy aimed at eliminating waste in processes.
LeSS	A methodology for scaled agile based on Scrum.
Multi-speed IT	Encapsulates the principle of different levels of agility in different types of systems, for example Pace Layering and Bi-modal IT.
MVP	A minimum viable product is the smallest feature set of a product that is required for initial go live with users.
Organisation	The business or enterprise seeking to deliver change and run technology products.
Pace Layering	A model for separation of systems that change at different rates and levels of agility. The common three layers are Systems of Innovation, Systems of Differentiation and Systems of Record.
Persona	A life like description of a real user of the product used by the team to gain greater insight into user needs.
Portfolio	The organisation's collection of technology products and services.

Term	Definition
Product	The combination of the technology and manual processes required to deliver a service to users.
Product Backlog	The prioritised list of User Stories to be delivered.
Product Board	Governance forum through which decisions outside of the remit of the Product Team are taken.
Product Increment	One of more features that have been added to the product for a release.
Product Owner	The individual who makes priority calls on change and determines the function of the Product.
Product Roadmap	A statement of intent with broad milestones and features for delivery.
Programme	A collection of several related change projects.
Project	A container for change to a product.
Release Sprint	A special purpose Sprint used to integrate the product with non-Agile changes elsewhere in the portfolio.
SAFe	The Scaled Agile Framework - a set of patterns and practices for Agile delivery.
Scrum	An Agile methodology for software delivery.
Service Team	A group of support analysts and engineers who resolve incidents in a live product.
Service Management	Management of the operational processes and support of a system typically in production.
Service Wrap	The set of manual processes, tools and technology that are used to run the product in a production environment and support the user.
Shear Layering	An Architectural principle that indicates that different aspects of a structure change at different rates.
Sprint	A time-boxed period for the delivery of change.
Sprint 0	A special purpose sprint used at the start of the Delivery phase to build and primes the delivery pipeline.

Term	Definition
Sprint Backlog	The list of User Stories to be delivered in a given Sprint.
Story	An element of change to be implemented in the Product.
Stream	A group of Teams working in a related functional or technical area.
'T' Individual	A team member with broad agile delivery experience coupled with a specialism.
TDA	Technical Design Authority - a body that meets to determine the best route forward for technical design decisions. It may be part of a generic Design Authority function.
TDD	Test Driven Development - a software engineering practice in which tests are written ahead of the software performing the function.
TQP	Technical Quality Plan - defines the practices required to maintain a high quality codebase.
User	An individual who uses the product.
Value	The benefit an organisation gains from implementing change and delivering a product to their customers.
XP	XP (eXtreme Programming) - a set of practices for Agile software development.